NONCOMPLIANT
A MEMOIR

BY
JENNIFER MARGUERITE

Acknowledgment

iii

I would like to acknowledge my husband, Anthony for always having my back and my children for loving me as I am. Also, thank you to Parker Publishing for taking a chance on an unknown and allowing me a venue for my voice.

"Last but not least, I wanna thank me I wanna thank me for believing in me I wanna thank me for doing all this hard work I wanna thank me for having no days off I wanna thank me for, for never quitting.

Snoop Dog

Dedication

For my Mother, Phyllis Edwards

You shaped me more than you know,

If only you were here on the earth

I would hug you tight and tell you so

I love you, ma. See you on the other side.

April 24, 2025

Media, Pa.

About the Author

Jennifer Marguerite still resides in Delaware County, Pa. just outside of Philadelphia. She graduated from Pennsylvania State University with a Bachelor of English and a minor in American Studies. Jennifer attended Eastern University for her Masters of Education program. She has been a public-school teacher for over 16 years. At home, Jennifer is content to spend time with her rescue dogs, Rolly and Scooby. She has been married to her husband Tony for 32 years. Together they have three adult children, and one grandson who is the light of their life.

Table of Contents

Chapter 1 3

Chapter 2 16

Chapter 3 29

Chapter 4 38

Chapter 5 52

Chapter 6 58

Chapter 7 75

Chapter 8 91

Chapter 9 98

Chapter 10 102

Chapter 11 108

Chapter 12 114

Chapter 13 124

Chapter 14 130

Chapter 15 138

Chapter 16 147

Chapter 17 154

Chapter 18 166

Chapter 19 173

Chapter 20 179

Chapter 21 184

Chapter 22 195

Chapter 23 198

Chapter 24 203

Chapter 25 206

Chapter 26 221

Chapter 27 229

Chapter 28 236

Chapter 29 242

Appendix 246

It was October of 2021 that my life went to complete crap. It's so hard to pinpoint the exact date or event that precipitated the spiral, because it wasn't just one isolated incident that led to my mental break. It was a culmination of family woes coupled with an incredible amount of work stress. My mental breakdown, as agonizing as it was, allowed me to grow exponentially as a person. Spirituality helped me to heal, and my ancestors played a part too. Luckily, I chronicled it all as it was unfolding, providing a glimpse inside the hell that is mental illness. Now, as a 54-year-old woman, I have discovered many ugly truths about myself and others. Never one to be silenced or marginalized, I have finally found my voice again. I firmly believe the issues I write about will resonate with others.

Perhaps the most infuriating thing I experienced during my mental lapse was how many speak to self-care and its importance. Yet, there is a huge disconnect between societal expectations and actual self-care. What's worse is that mental health is still somewhat taboo. Sure, your doctor will ask you about it; however, in reality, the state of mental health care in America is abysmal. Still, it's particularly frustrating that in this day and age, mental health resources are hard to find, difficult to navigate, and not readily available.

"Take care of yourself" is literally shoved down your throat on a daily basis. Meanwhile, in middle-class America, there is a crushing weight on the shoulders of most parents and professionals. Especially teachers. That's what I do – or did – for a living before it all came crashing down. As a teacher, I can state emphatically that we are far from prepared to handle the onslaught of mental health needs our students come to school with, and further on in the book, I will discuss the effect this is having on our schools, students, staff, and society in general.

This is a cautionary tale that blends aspects of the difficulties of parenting children, drawing boundaries (or in my case, the lack thereof), and the soul sucking societal expectations that cause much of our suffering. You will find that this book is heavily peppered with observations about the current climates of mental health and education in this country, and how I feel both are failing due to government dysfunction. More than anything, though, this chronicles my journey through the muck of mental illness, and how hard it was to get the help my family and I needed at a crucial time in our lives.

As far back as the year 1823, Lord Byron exclaimed in *Don Juan* that "'Tis strange-but true; for truth is always strange; Stranger than fiction…."

Indeed, the late great Mark Twain famously stated, "Truth is stranger than fiction because Fiction is obligated to stick to possibilities: Truth isn't." What follows on these pages is my truth.

Chapter 1

My story is a twisted one. It is raw, ugly, honest, and brutal, Kindreds.

I call you this because, if you are reading, then I suspect you are a kindred soul. A kindred spirit. An empath. They are all the same, basically. Labels are useless, for we are so much more than what we appear, than what we tend to show. Everyone has their gifts as well as their inner demons. What follows will detail mine.

To start with, I believe that whatever lingo you choose, life is concentric. Patterns repeat, coincidences don't exist, and kindred souls continually will seek to connect with other kindred souls. Evil is real, and it wears many faces. You only have to watch the nightly news to see the daily battle between good and evil. The latter sells, unfortunately.

When I was a kid growing up in the '70s and '80s, life was so completely different. There were no twenty-four-hour news outlets, no information highway. Cell phones, the Cloud, reality TV, none of it existed. We have all seen the memes, I assume, but living it was totally different.

We developed film at a pharmacy or drive-through drop-off. There weren't any selfies, so no instant gratification. Our parents couldn't reach us when we were out of the house, and we always had spare change for the pay phone. I fully acknowledge that I sound like an old person speaking. I guess I am ancient at 52. It feels like yesterday I was a young, pretty, energetic mom. It went fast. You hear people say that, but you don't know until here you are, a half a century old.

Which brings me back to the beginning. The beginning of my "adulthood," which I was completely unprepared for. I wasn't always a teacher. When I graduated from high school, I honestly didn't know what to do. Through teaching, I have found that many graduates don't. I didn't want to waste money on college since I had no idea what I wanted to be when I "grew up."

My mother's cousin was a partner in a salon in Southwest Philadelphia (Philly). She talked me into beauty school and gave me my first hairstylist gig. Sadly, she was murdered a few years later. (Alas, that is another story for a different day, Kindreds.) All told, I spent twenty years behind the chair, and it was a great job for a young mother. I could make my own schedule, so I worked a few nights and Saturday. That's when my husband, Tony, was off from work.

In this way, we were fortunate enough not to have to put our three young kids in daycare. The outrageous cost of childcare for three made it not worth going full-time, so my mom and mother-in-law helped out with babysitting. I never made a killing doing hair, just enough to put gas in the tank and money in the kids' lunch accounts. There were other ways to supplement, too, such as paper routes, and even hair on the side, despite it being considered illegal. My neighbors never narced me out, though, because I did their hair too! And yes, I drove around pregnant in my T-Bird stick shift at three in the morning, delivering the New York Times to rich people in Villanova and the Main Line. Whatever it takes has long been a mantra. I will admit, though, that later, when going through the throes of writing a senior thesis, I wished I had stayed at the salon. Yet, my arthritis and carpal tunnel were getting bad already, and I was only 35 then. What would I be like if I stayed on doing the exact same thing that was making me suffer?

Let it be known that I wouldn't trade being home with my kids when they were little for anything. We went to the zoo, museums, parks, arcades, the arboretum, and my mom's shore place several times a year. I found all the coupons and free passes I could, because it was expensive to entertain three young kids. We couldn't afford the outrageous cost of movies, and even when we did splurge, I was the mom sneaking candy in her purse.

In the morning, I would walk the dog to school with them. I began volunteering at their school, and that is how I fell in love with the classroom. School was so different from when I was a kid. You were actually encouraged to speak and share your mind. For an '80s kid who went through twelve years of Catholic schooling, this was revolutionary!

Life was so good then, I just didn't realize it. Time and life have a habit of getting away from you during the daily grind. It's ironic because most people's regret at the end is wasted time. However, I have found that when raising children, the days are long, but the years go fast.

While I would never consider time with my kids as wasted, we were stagnating. Most months, we robbed Peter to pay Paul, as the saying goes. I will never forget when my oldest, Angelica, came home from school and told me the playground aide said I can't layer her anymore, that she needed a winter jacket. What a shitty feeling – someone calling you out for being poor. She offered no help or assistance because we lived in a decent school district. That feeling of worthlessness, that stigma of "you are a bad parent" without it actually being said, is what drove me to seek new avenues.

After sixteen years in the trade, I started really pondering my future. I had no retirement fund, no health benefits, and I was already 35. If the next couple of decades went as fast as the previous, I would find myself unprepared. I didn't want to be an old woman eating cat food.

So, when my youngest, Ella, went off to first grade, I went off to college. I enrolled at Penn State University, but I attended a satellite campus in my hometown. It was an awesome experience. I learned so much more because I was finally ready to do so.

It took five years, but I graduated as a Jane Cooper Scholar with a BA in English and a minor in American Studies. Immediately upon graduating, I enrolled in a Master's program in Multicultural Education, which was also accompanied by a teaching certification program. All told, I was in college for eight years straight! It was one of the most challenging things I have ever accomplished. I attended school full-time, worked part-time, and raised a family while maintaining a 3.8 grade point average. When attending Eastern University for my dual program, I was working full-time as a Special Education Para. After gaining my certification and Master's degree, I subbed for a while until I landed my dream job. The position was in a 1-8 building, so I got the best of both worlds! I taught middle school reading intervention, and I also pulled young students from grades 1, 2, 3, and 4, depending on need.

It was refreshing to have my confidence restored by the "littles" after being with the middle school kids. Teachers are rock stars when you are in elementary school, and not so much in middle school. Regardless, I was able to make really deep connections with the middle school students. I became the "go-to" for many of our more troubled kids. It was a role I craved, as it fulfilled something in me that had been missing since my own children were mostly grown by then.

For the first few years, I was on a honeymoon with my job. I couldn't do enough for my school. I became the PBIS Co–Coach, a Student Council Moderator, and a mentor for both new teachers and older students. I was fully and totally committed to this school. I loved teaching reading, I loved my students, and life was really good.

Sometimes, taking one positive and running with it opens up many other doors. I was feeling professionally fulfilled at work, and that attitude of success came home with me every day. For a while, at least.

Fast forward three years. The teaching shortage – you know the one no one wants to address, let alone fix – came into play. It became increasingly difficult to find substitute teachers. My groups were being canceled weekly so that I could chip in with the sub situation. We limped through most of the year that way, until March, when a sixth-grade teacher went out on medical leave for the remainder of the school year.

Again, subs were being plugged in. However, we were in the middle of the required state standardized testing, so subs were obtained through a staffing agency. Odd how subs were to be found then, but not after testing was complete. Ironic how that works, isn't it? (Insert sarcasm) Not to mention, where did the sub money go when we were unable to obtain them?

If you guessed that I was put in that room for the remainder of the year, you would be correct, Kindreds. My groups of intensive reading support were canceled, meaning those students got zero extra help. Please note that these students read significantly below grade level. Sometimes they are several grade levels below. Why then is this an acceptable practice? And were the parents aware? Teachers walk a tightrope between "towing the company line" and being honest with parents and guardians.

By the time I was placed in that classroom, it was a zoo. Months of no routine and little instruction had rendered that class unmanageable. In fact, they had conspired to get the last long-term sub fired. I think that was their plan with me as well, but I am a little harder to reach. The class was unruly, disrespectful, and sometimes downright violent. They would throw things, yell curses, and just disrupt the class constantly. One day, a girl brought a bottle of perfume to homeroom and went around spraying it in all the boys' eyes. Has anyone tried to take a glass bottle away from a large 6th grader who is faster than you? All while choking on perfume? It was not a highlight of my career. Although the real shame of it was that there were about a dozen students out of the thirty who really wanted to learn, but they couldn't. They were unable to hear me teaching over the noise and chaos. I bought a microphone. I showed interesting videos. I gave out "dollars" for the school store to those who followed expectations, hoping it would entice others to get on board. It didn't. I stepped up my game and started distributing emoji tickets in addition to the dollars. I pulled a winner each day who got to choose from my prize box. (Which I fund out of my own pocket.)

Alas, nothing worked long-term. The students who wanted to sabotage the class continued to do so. I continued to try to teach over them. It was a mess. Those kids had gone so long without regular instruction and clear expectations that I couldn't get them back on track. All of this in addition to the fact that I wasn't even teaching in my certification area. I was teaching Medieval European History.

Every night, I would go home and review the material so that I could teach the students the next day. The last week of school, I was asked to grade a semester's worth of papers and calculate, then post grades for the entire 6th-grade class – well over 90 students. I was promised to be paid for my time. I never was.

I left school that year feeling a mixture of relief, exhaustion, and trepidation. Was this how it would go again next year? It is truly demoralizing to work so hard with your own students and start to see real learning gains, just to have it all wiped away so you can babysit. I do not mean to be offensive, but that's what it was. Glorified babysitting. All I could do was keep these kids alive. I was rendered ineffective and that is a horrible feeling for a person committed to furthering students of high poverty. I have personally witnessed how low socio-economic schools are continually underfunded and understaffed, while maintaining high administrative salaries. I can assertively maintain through my experience lasting almost a decade, that children of poverty are constantly and consistently not receiving services that they are entitled to by law. Imagine my disillusionment, if you will, for a minute. I attended school as a middle-aged adult, hoping to find my dream job to enjoy every day until retirement. Yet, here I was a building sub. That's back where I had started, basically. The cruelest part was that under the right leadership, I was thriving, and so were my students. We operated our Intervention like a finely tuned machine, largely in part due to my work bestie, Liz. This allowed us to serve as many children as possible.

Shortly after the start of the next school year, one of our young 5th-grade teachers got very ill. We had a rotation of teachers, like myself, going in there, but with no steady adult presence day in and day out, the students were brutal. It was a repeat of the previous year. Relationships matter, Kindreds. Students work harder for teachers they know and like.

One day, a fistfight broke out between two fifth-grade boys. One student was very small and the other quite large. I called the emergency number, like we are supposed to in this situation. No one answered. I called again, same deal. I then called the office to ask for help.

In the meantime, these kids are pummeling each other, and every other student is screaming. I had to step in and stop it. I was trying to separate them when I took a punch to the temple that knocked me off balance, and I fell. By then, the cavalry had arrived, but it was already over. I went home that night, sore and demoralized. I immediately went to bed. The next morning, I felt worse. I was dizzy, off balance, and my back was in agony. I went to work and talked to the school nurse. She gave me paperwork to fill out. It was for workers' compensation. I didn't want to go out on leave or anything; I just needed a doctor.

The doctor was a quack. He prescribed meds that made me so out of it I could barely drive, let alone be in charge of a classroom. So I went back. He cut the meds in half and prescribed Physical Therapy. The meds were still an issue, as I don't typically take anything stronger than ibuprofen. Plus, the hours that this therapy was offered were the same exact hours I worked.

Yet, the district wanted me to use my sick time to attend. Excuse me, but wasn't I hurt on the job? As I said, I didn't want anything other than to get better. It was a battle, and one I didn't need since I was in a battle most days in the classroom.

Eventually, they relented and allowed me to be 30 minutes late on days I had therapy. I went through two PT courses and wasn't any better. A visit to my own family doctor seemed in order, and they prescribed testing. I underwent that and found out I had Degenerative Disc Disease in my spine. A chiropractor was recommended.

When I first met with Dr. Dave, he explained that a "life event" such as a car accident or an injury like mine precipitated the degeneration. I attended sessions with the chiropractor three times a week for a year before I felt any better. I still have to go every three weeks for treatment. It was literally a life-long injury.

Meanwhile, the situation at school continued to deteriorate. One day, I had to disarm a student who was going after a girl with a razor knife! When I turned the weapon over, I was asked by the admin why I took it upon myself to disarm the student, as opposed to calling the emergency number.

"You mean the one I called before, and no one answered?" I sweetly responded.

Needless to say, by the time the pandemic had arrived, we were beyond burnt out. Our governor ordered all schools closed. Each district made the move to online schooling. Our online learning was limited to a platform where students submitted their work. I was tasked with contacting the parents and guardians of the 5th-grade students who did not complete their work.

This was insurmountable because the adults in many of our students' lives just didn't place a high value on education. Can I blame them? As you can see, socio-economically challenged students are always getting the short end of the stick. Not to mention, they also distrusted institutions. Once again, this is through no fault of their own. (Think Tuskegee) The current (and past) administration has failed us time and time again, both at the local and federal levels. Add in the mess the state has made of education, and I completely understand the disengagement.

Additionally, it's really hard to worry about assignments or homework when you are trying to keep the lights on. We have students who literally spend their nights in the dark or babysit their siblings while their parents or guardians work. A large percentage of our student body got the best seven hours of their day when they were with us.

All of our students received free lunch and breakfast at school, because many came from food-insecure homes. We distributed food care packages at the school during the pandemic, but unless a child could walk or get a ride, they wouldn't receive them. Additionally, when schools were shuttered, many parents lost their childcare. This led to unemployment and more homelessness. COVID robbed all of us, Kindreds.

Summer was weird that year, also thanks to COVID. Who could forget the toilet paper shortages? Shows and concerts were canceled, household supplies were scarce, and many states were on lockdown. There were so many conflicting reports about COVID, the spread of it, and the fatalities due to it. Disinformation flowed, both on television and the internet – and the general public ate it all up. Interstate travel was restricted in many areas, and quarantine was mandated after a trip. My mom, who had weathered the winters in a little trailer in Florida since she retired, was stuck down there. Unfortunately, my stepfather suffered from the same back ailment as I did. However, he was in the late stages before he sought help. He maintained that old school machismo that just grates me the wrong way. Men like him don't go to the doctor because, in their warped perception, that is like admitting a weakness.

Since he had ignored the problem for so long, he needed surgery. He was scheduled to have it at the Veterans Administration hospital in Florida. So Mom was unable to leave. The majority of the world was hunkered down at this time anyhow. It is worth mentioning that strong women have raised me to be a strong woman. My mom had married this dude shortly after my dad died. He lived in 1950. When he moved in, I was a teenager. He swooped in and crashed our party. My mom was a free spirit. We were raised to respect, but also have fun.

Suddenly, we had to ask to be excused from dinner. My brothers were forbidden from wearing ball caps at the table, but he could show up wearing no shirt. If that wasn't the most unappetizing thing ever, I don't know what was.

Plus, my mother had to serve him. All while he denigrated her. For the life of me, I will never understand why she put up with it. I despised him, as did most of my siblings. Those were hard years, real hard. The kind of hard you never want for your own children. Meanwhile, he had four of his own in another state, which he barely acknowledged. Go figure.

As summer gives way to fall, many schools attempt to reopen amidst the pandemic. Social distancing in classrooms, cafeterias, and on school buses was mandatory, as were masks. Schools with high enrollments had to switch between students being present in the classroom and maintaining an online presence when some students were at home. It was, to say the least, difficult. And contact tracing was a downright nightmare! I know of districts that deliberately fudged the numbers to be able to stay open. The switch to a totally online system was so tedious; this was the loophole for many.

Our district was the only school in the state of Pennsylvania to decide to remain virtual for the entire school year. We didn't even attempt to open. I knew we couldn't do it safely, but I also recognized that many of our students were safer at school. I worked my butt off to make sure students had what they needed to be successful online. My sixth graders learned about Mythology in our class that year, and they really ran with it. Each student created their own mythological character that was a child of a Greek God. They wrote short origin stories about their character, accompanied by an illustration.

Some of these were hand-drawn, others were digital. I created books from these tales and gifted each student one. I still have mine. Their originality was incredible. Low income does not equate to low intelligence!

The following fall, we came back to in-person learning. It was difficult to recognize students with masks on, and they had trouble hearing us with the masks on. Our students had been out of a classroom for a year and a half. Imagine how long that is in kid years, Kindreds.

Needless to say, it was starting from scratch. We did the best we could with the limited resources we had. I know the Biden administration showered schools with money for COVID-19 learning, but I would be hard-pressed to say where any of it went. I think my administration would be too.

We navigated the ups and downs of having a student body of over 600 in one building. Many of our students were experiencing trauma from having lost close family members to COVID or from losing housing when school went virtual and childcare was closed. Plus, our classrooms and bathrooms were not being cleaned properly. But, by all means, a mask will protect you! Throw in the fact that a shooting occurred at our opening high school football game, killing a 6-year-old student in our district. I knew returning would be a shit show, but our administration outdid every expectation I had, and not in a good way. This same upper administration recommended self-care along with securing social-emotional best practices for our kids. No resources were offered, no time to develop this, just the decree from above.

In a building as large as ours, one would expect counseling services to be offered. However, we had one counselor for all those students, and she was drowning. We were all drowning. Once teachers and staff started contracting COVID, it was time to cue up the teacher merry-go-round. In the past, we had collapsed classes and split pupils up between existing grade level teachers when we were totally desperate for staff. Yet, COVID guidelines prohibited that practice. Further, students were being sent home with COVID-19 symptoms, only to return to the classroom the following day. This left us in a dire predicament. Once again, Kindreds, reading classes were canceled. *I mean, come on, how well do students really need to know how to read? It's not likely many of ours will go to college anyhow.*

If you find this offensive, bullseye! So do I, but this was the prevailing attitude of our administrators. You know, the administrators who make six figures? In a low-income school district, to boot.

In fact, not only did we have administrators who kept their heads buried in the sand instead of doing their jobs, we also had no subs, no Social Emotional Resources, an incomplete curriculum, canceled Prep periods, canceled reading classes, broken buildings, subpar professional development, and a counselor ratio of one to 600. Not to mention, our tech didn't work with everyone in the building who was using it. Not enough bandwidth or something.

When you are an empath, or whatever term you use for people like me, you tend to feel things much more deeply: sadness, regret, guilt, shame, despondency, rebellion. Our hallways were filled with all the feelings I was internalizing. These students needed more than we had to give. With what limited resources and staff we had, everyone was barely hanging on. This is a recipe for disaster, as you will later see.

The weary trudged on. When I say this, it is not to tug at the heartstrings and demand more accountability, although that would be nice. It is meant to illustrate that our kids were just as taxed as we were. Of course, they felt the pinch. Aforementioned, this was the best seven hours of their day. That became no longer the case.

Moreover, it was unbelievably insulting to be taxed beyond what is feasible and possible at work, but then receive emails from the Human Resources department reminding us to be vigilant of self-care and practice mindfulness. I would be wise to remind you that this was the same department that was responsible for filling vacancies and establishing reliable sub-services. The disconnect was impossible to comprehend. While teachers were burning the candle at both ends, so to speak, the administrators were sleeping. It reminded me of that story about the napping dragon guarding the gold.

As is always the case in situations that are unjust, people were upset. I was one of them. We couldn't properly staff our building, let alone safely! Teachers have unions, my Kindreds. Almost everyone knows that. What they don't know is that the vast majority of them are weak. Sure, you will see the teachers on strike for better wages or teaching conditions on the news, but in reality, very few tow that line and actually go on strike. Our union president was in her last tenure before retiring. She grieved complaints as she got them. Grievances are a unionized way of filing a concrete complaint that must be addressed. I couldn't even begin to imagine how many she must have filed last year, as I was in the building before taking leave.

Our other reading teacher saw the writing on the wall and offered to take over a sixth-grade English Language Arts class whose teacher was going out on maternity leave. At least that was in her discipline. This was another job they failed to post. I mean, c'mon – this isn't a sudden illness! It's maternity leave. Human Resources (HR) knew about this for months upon months. At least the other reading teacher wouldn't have that nagging anxiety in the pit of her stomach that we all had for months now, driving into work. Where will I be today? What am I teaching? Why did I burn hours this weekend doing planning that is useless?

All teachers acknowledge that children are creatures of habit, so we tailor our time with that in mind. We perform routines every day that help students feel safe and at ease. Routines are predictable, and in our student's lives, not much else was. Cohesiveness was of the utmost importance, and we simply didn't have it. It irked me until it inflamed me.

Meanwhile, I was being plugged into classrooms more often than I had my own kids. Mind you, I had second graders who didn't know the alphabet! I hope you read that twice, Kindreds, staring and not believing or comprehending those words in front of you. The pandemic learning gap is real, and ours was way larger because we spent a full eighteen months online. Additionally, our reading teachers were subbing and not teaching, so low readers were certainly not going to close that gap. Our district had essentially no plan to address this issue. I will ask again, why is this acceptable? What I would soon realize, much to my chagrin, is that no one cared enough to speak up.

Chapter 2

Life went on. So did the rollercoaster that I found myself on daily. As I mentioned earlier, I have three adult children. Our oldest, Angelica, blessed us with our first grandchild, a boy named Kaleb. That child is the reason I am still here.

My son Aaron had moved out that fall, and we only had my youngest, Ella, at home. She was a young adult, working for the same company Tony did. He was an HVAC tech, but so much more. One time when the power was out for days, he rigged something up to my Jeep, and we had lights at least. Tony could basically fix anything, so he was a hot commodity at work. However, he had blown his knee out on a job and had surgery. He was upstate convalescing that fall. I got a call one night when I was home alone, sleeping. It was Angelica, and she was hysterically screaming. I couldn't understand her. In the background, I could hear baby daddy screaming and banging. I heard one desperate "Mom help!" before the phone went dead.

Of course, I jumped out of bed and ran out the back door wearing nothing but pajamas and slippers. I wanted to call 911, but couldn't remember her house number – I was in such a panic. I raced down Interstate 95. For once in my life, I wanted a police officer to pull me over! My daughter lives just 20 minutes down I-95 from me. It was the longest 20 minutes of my life. I arrived to find her and the baby in the living room, both crying. The house was a mess. Her partner had blown up and put his hands on her. He had punched walls and the bathroom door. We cleaned up as thoroughly as possible, packed a bag for each of them, and left. I lay in bed that night trying to calm down my terrified grandson. He just shook and cried. My heart broke for him. I just wanted to protect this helpless little bundle of love, but all I could do was douse the blaze. If you guessed she went back to him, you would be correct, Kindreds. Love is love, right?

By Halloween, Tony was home, and all seemed semi-well. Work still sucked, and unfortunately, I brought it home with me. I've never been good at drawing healthy boundaries. Yeah, I know, it's not self-care. That phrase alone makes me want to gouge my own eyes out. However, I have to admit that the worst was getting that email from HR with the subject line blaring "Self Care Is Important!" Or "Self Care Is Necessary!" Sometimes they would change it up to "Take Time for You!"

My personal favorite was the year they sponsored a "Walk to the Summit" fitness challenge. Up for grabs were "treasures" such as gift cards, tumblers, you know the drill.

Most ironic is that this was sponsored at the same time that teachers were conducting state testing, which is a nightmare unto itself. So yeah, sure, come walk during the only bathroom or food break you get. How out of touch can you be with the needs of the buildings in your district that you supposedly serve? To add insult to injury, they had time for that nonsense, but not to post jobs?

It still bears repeating, though, that in a high-poverty, underperforming school, we only had three reading teachers for over 600 students! Now, one was placed as a long-term sub for the year, meaning her students received zero support. I was the next in line to be placed, and we had another 6th-grade teacher who was expecting a child.

What do you suppose Human Resources did about this, Kindreds? Nothing, of course. I feel like my teacher is really showing – I keep posing questions and looking for answers while writing this. Sometimes there aren't any answers. Or none that we like anyhow.

To say this became a hamster wheel of dysfunction is putting it mildly. Our job is to move kids. Bring in the lowest group, give them what they need, and then transition them back to the classroom to move onto the next lowest group. Wash, rinse, repeat. Our reading spots were competitive, because yet once again, the need outweighed the available resources and staff. When done properly (and fully staffed), this program is very successful. At our school, the issue was no longer due to the subbing. For the life of me, I couldn't fathom how our district was okay with this. But no response is a response in itself, isn't it?

November held many surprises for me, none of which were pleasant. At the beginning of the month, I got a call at work. It had started as a good day. I actually didn't have to sub, and the students were so happy to see me; they really worked hard. I look back and feel wistful about it because my days were numbered. I mostly feel sad because it was one of the last good days we had together. My little community would soon disintegrate due to subbing. I can't emphasize enough how depressing, dispiriting, and downright defeating that school year was.

Anyhow, I got the call at lunch. It was the police. They had taken my son, Aaron, to the hospital. Apparently, he was experiencing a mental crisis. The police informed me that he had called them himself. He told them that his roommate (his childhood best friend) was raping and murdering girls, and he could hear him dragging the bodies around, but he couldn't figure out where they were hidden. I shakily grabbed my purse. What the hell was happening? This was my son, the honors student who had graduated from college Magna Cum Laude. I couldn't wrap my mind around it. I was terrified and stupefied. So I went to my building principal and told him I had a family emergency and had to leave for the day. He understood. I rushed to the hospital – and called Tony as I was pulling out of the school parking lot. I gave him the abbreviated version, and he agreed to meet me there.

When we arrived, the guard directed us to a nurse's station. When the nurse asked us what we needed, I informed her that the police had called and said that they were bringing my adult child in. She responded, "No, they didn't."

I said, "Excuse me?"

She told me that "He wasn't there yet."

In retrospect, I never told her my adult child was a male. She directed us to a waiting room, and there we sat – the two of us – twiddling our thumbs, sitting on pins so to speak. The police had cautioned me that due to COVID, all hospitals with a psych ward were on diversion. The local community hospital didn't have the right resources he would need, but at least this was a start. So there we sat. A million thoughts were running through my mom's mind: What if he really did hear a crime during its commission? What if he committed a crime? Was he on drugs? If so, what kind? How do I help him? I admit freely to having an overactive imagination. Yet, show me one mom who, in that situation, wouldn't be going stir-crazy! We sat for about 45 minutes.

That same nurse who lied to my face and told me my son wasn't there finally came out. She let us know that he signed himself out against medical advice (meaning insurance won't pay, but that was the least of my worries!)

I remember saying to her, "But he is in crisis! Why would you ever let him sign himself out?"

She smiled sweetly and told me she was very sorry, but he is an adult and can do as he likes. Tony looked about ready to boil over, so I rushed him towards the door. We drove around looking for him. He was on foot, so that he couldn't have gotten very far. When we finally found him, he ran. Tony was yelling out the car window at him while I was driving. Aaron finally relented and got in the car.

"Where are you taking me?" was his first question.

I knew he was afraid we would 302 him. For those of you who are not familiar with a 302, it is used when a person is a danger to themselves or others. With a 302, the person experiencing a mental health crisis is involuntarily committed, meaning they are taken against their will and placed in a psychiatric unit. Just imagine how traumatizing this is to a person who is already in a heightened state of crisis.

We managed to get him to our house, and I fed him something. I hadn't realized how much weight he had lost. After that, we got him situated on the couch, and I went about the business of calling doctors and trying to secure him medication. Three years ago, Aaron was diagnosed as schizophrenic. It has been a whirlwind of ups and downs with him, his meds, his doctors, and his jobs ever since. He had stopped seeing his last psychiatrist because she overmedicated him, and he almost had a stroke. In his mind, it made sense to go from too many meds to none at all.

Again, it was next to impossible to get him help when he was considered an adult. While I was on the phone, Aaron ran away. He threw his SIM card in the bushes and took off. Ella saw him running down the street. I hopped in the car to chase him down, and both Tony and Ella left on foot. Tony was hobbling on crutches, still not completely healed from surgery.

Luckily, I found Aaron about six blocks away. When he saw me, he turned to run the other way. I followed, keeping pace.

"This only ends one of two ways," I told him out the car window, "either you end up in jail or the hospital."

This made him pause. He stood staring, his eyes wild. He reminded me of a caged animal, and my heart broke for him. I was so helpless to help him, and that is the worst feeling ever for a mother.

Finally, he relented. I watched as the fight seemed to drain out of him. He stared straight down, not making eye contact. His shoulders sagged. He got in the back seat and immediately asked again: "Where are you taking me?"

I responded, "To find your dad and sister."

We found them, and then we headed home. Tony turned to Aaron and softly asked, "Where did you think you were going, bud?"

"To start a new life with my two dollars," Aaron replied, staring out the window.

When we arrived back home, Aaron was extremely agitated. He refused to sit and just paced around the first floor of the house, talking to himself. It was decided that Tony and I would take turns sleeping and keeping watch over him. He was freaking me out with the thousand-yard stare, mumbling to himself, and pacing constantly. His eyes were completely black. There was no color left to them anymore. I was afraid – both for him and of him. I advised Ella to lock her bedroom door when she retired for the evening. She sadly shook her head, "Yes." It was unbelievable, this is where we were.

Eventually, he snuck out again and took an Uber home. He wouldn't answer our calls, so Angelica drove there. He refused to let her in and said he just wanted to rest.

My son was in crisis for almost a month. We took turns keeping an eye on him. It takes a really, painfully long time for a person to come down from that severe of a mental health crisis. Aaron was supremely lucky to have parents and sisters who worked their arses off to help him. Many of those suffering from mental health issues don't have that support system.

At his worst, my son thought his father and I hated him, wanted him dead, and had contracted someone to "put a hit on him." Those are his words, not mine. It was immensely hurtful to have your child think that, while his family was the only people trying to help him. It took multiple appointments, phone calls, and prescriptions to get him back. It absolutely got worse before it got better, but we did get through it.

My point in all of this negative personal narrative is that it was nearly impossible to get my son the help he needed. He was an adult, but he had schizophrenia. He distrusted everyone – doctors, medical professionals, police, ambulance personnel, and me: us, his family. HIPAA is wonderful, in essence, but it does not further actually help the mentally ill. Something needs to change. Sure, my son could have signed a Power of Attorney that allowed us to make his medical decisions, but let us acknowledge that the biggest symptom of his disease is paranoia. He was never giving us that power, as he thought we had a "hit" on him.

Oddly enough, that particular idea never seemed to dissipate completely, even when he came down from the crisis. My heart hurt knowing my son was hearing things and maybe even seeing things, and only medication could curb it. Because Kindreds, this isn't Covid. Or a cold. Nor is it the flu. Mental illness is a lifelong condition. There is no getting better. There is only management.

By December of that year, I was pulled almost the daily. Imagine, if you will, what the vibe in our school was. Teachers weren't getting prep periods. That meant spending lunch gathering all the materials and resources needed to teach the next portion of the day. We all ate on the run …. Or survived on pure caffeine. Teachers were beyond burnt. The copiers jammed constantly because they were used, leased machines. Therefore, any grading or parental contact had to be done after hours. The lowest performing students of these teachers were no longer receiving reading services. This typically led to misbehavior because these students were bored and frustrated – the content was over their heads. When kids aren't engaged in a whole group atmosphere, they tend to cause problems and act out. This is because they are lost and disconnected from both the content and the group.

What child deserves to feel this way at school? Let's consider that no reading teacher is helping these students acquire the skills to close the reading gap. These children were being set up for failure. So were we teachers. Moreover, non-homeroom teachers were bitter and pitted against each other because no one wanted to be the one to get pulled. I was tagged in on Friday, December 10th, and informed that I would be the go-to from now on. I wanted to cry. I didn't, though, and managed to muster through.

These students were seventh graders. I had many of them the year we were online due to the pandemic. Homeroom went well. I took roll, collected lunch orders, and managed homework, including missing assignments and notes on absences or early dismissals. I sent each to where it went. Then, students went row by row to their lockers. I typically like to mix things up and keep it more interesting than this mundane routine, but I needed to form a cohesive unit first.

Honestly, those who aren't in education just don't get the amount of elements and work that actually goes into it. You have to be on every second of the day. It is exhausting, but also, oh so very rewarding. Further, I had built relationships with many of these kids during the COVID crisis. I had taught some of these students reading when they were in the younger grades, and I had also taught a few of their older siblings. I felt the first drop of optimism in I don't know how long.

That was short-lived. A student in the first period had a PCA.

For those not down with the public-school lingo, this is a Personal Care Assistant. She was a pretty, young black woman. I really liked her, and so did her student assignee. The first portion of the instruction went well. It all went downhill when the students broke into small groups. This is a best practice in education. The idea behind small groups is that students can work collaboratively to dive deeper into the content just presented. The teacher circulates the room, guiding and assisting in furthering the learning objective.

While doing this, a pencil comes flying across the room. It was a good shot – I will give him that. It sailed a centimeter across the nose of the beloved PCA and hit the locker behind her. I saw where it came from, but I just couldn't prove it. All I could do was break that group up and make them work independently while I hovered. Not soon enough, the lunch bell rang. The students lined up, at least a sub's semblance of a line, and off we went.

Our classroom was at the top of a long hallway, so we had to make our way down to the cafeteria. Classes were changing, students were yelling, and teachers and aides with raised voices were trying to herd the crowds. It was sensory overload for me, so I can only imagine how overwhelming it must have been for our students. Our school was taxed to its limits; we were bursting at the seams. Our enrollment far exceeded the ability of our 50+ year-old building. Kids' shoulders brushed against each other in the hallway. It was inevitable, but according to our students' loose rules, this could be construed as a reason to fight. We had made it to the cafeteria, but our tables weren't cleaned and ready. Again, we are perpetually understaffed. If you have worked in a school in the month of December, you know well the special kind of crazy that prevails. If run properly, teachers and administration can harness that energy for the positive: food and clothes drives, community outreach, and candy sales. None of this could have happened with us because of the staffing issues. The prevailing vibe at our school had become overwhelmingly negative by this point.

As we waited outside the cafe, an 8th-grade girl came down the hallway with a hall pass. Ordinarily, she would have been able to get a drink up by the 8th-grade classrooms, but that fountain was broken. This was the norm. Many bathrooms were typically closed due to sewage backups. In fact, the cafe has been known to back up with raw sewage, but hey, don't let that stop lunch. The boy I knew had thrown a pencil earlier; now he threw a marker full force at this girl. Luckily, his aim was off, or it would have hit her in the face. Instead, it hit the wall behind her and shattered. She screamed, and the loud, hot hallway suddenly seemed silent.

It was as if we all took a collective breath, and time hovered. The student in question stood staring defiantly at me, his nostrils flaring. His eyes were huge and his face red. His hands were so large that I hadn't even seen the marker he clutched, although I made him line leader, mostly so I could monitor him. All to no avail. I said his name gently and asked him to go wait on the bench by the office for me. It was the only reasonable, non-inflammatory response that could be given, given the circumstances.

This student was a year behind and should have been in 8th grade. He was big for even an 8th grader. His family had been at war with the district for years about his special education designation. The kid was in 7th grade and couldn't read. Both his parents and the system were failing him, and he was in the wrong placement. His frustration was supreme and it was coming out as violent outbursts. His strength was scary as opposed to impressive.

As we waited for his reply, he began clenching his fists, furled and unfurled, the whole time staring at me with those giant, rage-filled eyes. I don't know what he saw when he looked at me that day – the parents who failed him due to their misplaced pride, the teachers who handed him an iPad instead of a book. This administration not only allowed this to go on but also suspended him almost weekly.

Perhaps he simply saw a white woman who had no idea what it was like to be him, and as loving as she was, he didn't identify with her. He was the kid who needed a friend, and never had one. He was the bully and the victim. He was being failed, and on too many levels to count. At that point, the bubble burst. I felt the air leave the hallway and return. Suddenly, the noise was back, students were screaming, and security swooped in. I watched him being dragged away as I led the students to their tables. That was when my dam burst.

After I got the students seated, I went to my classroom. It was dark and desolate, just like me. I sat at my desk that was overflowing with data that I wouldn't be bothering to share, because these students – like so many before them – were not getting any help for the rest of the year. They would languish in a classroom, not having any idea what they were looking at. Behavior issues will ensue. I soaked my desk calendar with tears. At some point, our head maintenance lady, Doll, came in. She offered no words; she just hugged me. It was what I needed to get through the day, and I am eternally grateful to her. The maintenance staff, secretaries, aides, PCAs, cafeteria crew, crossing guards, and bus drivers are invaluable. It truly does take a village. Yet, those who turn the public education wheel (which feels more like a boulder) are so undervalued. Not only that, but we are all underpaid.

After I got myself to the point I wasn't sobbing, just leaking and gibbering, I went to my building principal. He was a cool guy, but a horrible leader. I told him I needed to think about it over the weekend, but I might resign or take a leave. He did his usual "I am your best friend" routine, which is supposed to fix everything in his feeble mind. Did I mention he was a gym teacher? No offense to those teachers, but this dude was the archetype of a dumb hunk. He had no business being a principal. A flash of his "boyish" grin and some mumbled words were the antidote. This makes sense, no?

Alas, he was transferred around instead of being terminated, and was now at our school. It was outrageous, dysfunctional, and disgusting. I felt a fire brewing in my belly.

When the bell rang at 3:20, I was beyond relieved. I packed and left, making no stops in the parking lot to chat with a colleague or on the way home to run my payday errands. I was so exhausted and just fundamentally sad and defeated to my core. Tony and I were going upstate to get a Christmas tree that weekend. I drove to the mountains with my dogs in tow, and I don't remember a second of it. In retrospect, who the hell let me behind the wheel that night? I am stubborn, and so if I am honest, I have no one to blame but myself. Who wants to fight with a headstrong woman on the brink of collapse?

We woke up on Saturday and set out to find the perfect tree. My situation at school was super heavy on my mind. Tears leaked out of my eyes. I tried to be present in the moment, but all I could think of was Monday. This was not going to go well. I had once again been set up for failure. We were only about five minutes into the ride when the first waves hit. All of a sudden, I couldn't breathe. I clawed at my neck, willing my airway to open. It didn't. I motioned for Tony to pull over. I literally fell out of the truck and landed on my knees. I was still clawing at my throat, and now I could feel the bile rising. "I'm going to choke!" was my first thought. It was quickly followed by "This must be what dying is like. I am having a heart attack and dying here on the side of the road."

I am always my own worst enemy – none of these realizations did anything to quell my panic. Yet, the knowledge that my dad had died of a massive heart attack much younger than I currently am did nothing to dissipate the feeling that my chest was caving in and I was losing my grasp on the here and now.

At this point, I was crawling on my hands and knees. It was as if I could get away from what was happening to me. Just as dots were beginning to blur my vision, I started hearing a hornet's nest buzzing loudly. It didn't register then that there are no bees in the mountains of Pennsylvania in December. I tried to look around – an insect attack was not on my list of things to do that day. I couldn't see properly, but I discovered I could now breathe. I took in the air with big, gusting breaths. That only caused me to throw up.

There I was retching when Tony finally got out of the truck and helped me to my feet. He guided me back to the truck. I was still spitting the foul taste of vomit out of my mouth, while continuing to fill my lungs with deep, whooshing gulps of air.

Certainly, I looked like road kill. My hair was wild, I had mud all over my pants and hands, I had used my dirty hands to claw my neck, and I had tears and snot flowing down my face. I didn't dare look in the side-view mirror. I knew I wouldn't recognize the reflection.

Tony got me situated, buckled in, and found me some napkins. I cleaned up the best I could, but my breathing remained harsh and ragged. I was what my young adult children would call "tweaking." I was jumping out of my own skin, and everything was too much. When I say "everything," that is to say, the heat in the truck was too hot, the sun was too bright, the radio was too loud, and the exhaust was overwhelming my already distraught lungs.

I didn't realize it at the time, but I was experiencing one hell of a panic attack.

We still went and got a tree that day. I pushed through, which is typical for me.

What was not typical is that I don't remember much of that afternoon. Nor that evening. We had plans to go to my mom's that night for dinner and drinks. My brother was going to be there, and I was really looking forward to it. Tony says I got home and helped him get the tree in the stand, and then I sat on the couch. He said I just sat there, staring off into space. I didn't respond to him or any other stimuli. I apparently sat there until I fell asleep, and I never woke until the next day.

Looking back, it is just one more thing my school district robbed me of: dinner with my mother. It may seem such a small matter; however, none of us knew then that in two months' time, Mom would be dead.

Chapter 3

I called out of work on Monday and went to see my family practitioner. She was actually a CRNP, and the doctor she worked under was someone I had never met. Neither had Tony, and we had been with this particular family practice for years. It was odd, but we received good care, so neither of us gave a fig. I explained to the CRNP what had happened. For the sake of argument, we will call her Lena. I was crying as I recounted my saga. She gave me a note to stay out of work for two weeks. She also prescribed Zoloft. I was to follow up in two weeks' time. I don't remember much about those two weeks, except that I was on autopilot – wrapping gifts, baking cookies, and cleaning. But some days I didn't bother showering or brushing my teeth. Self-care looks different for everyone.

My self-care at that time was simply surviving. I continued with panic attacks, but on a smaller scale. My GI issues were insane, and I could not venture far from a bathroom. Yet, Christmas was coming, and the whole family was going to the mountains to celebrate with my mom. I had to muster through, and thank God I did, since it was her very last Christmas on this side of earth.

That holiday wasn't perfect; it was chaotic and messy, but we owned it. I have always said, "My family puts the fun in dysfunction." We did have fun, but my mom definitely didn't look good. Her legs were all swollen and leaking. You see, Kindreds, my mother had been diagnosed with a rare disease called "Good Pastures." I don't know why it is named that, since there is nothing good about it.

Essentially, your body makes antibodies that attack your lungs and kidneys. I don't think it is fully understood yet, because as I said, it is rare. According to the Cleveland Clinic's website states, "there are fewer than two cases per one million people." (https://my.clevalandclinic.org)

Back in 2010, my mom collapsed in the bathroom one Sunday afternoon. It was a month before she was released from the hospital. She was diagnosed with those good pastures thing that wasn't good. She was in and out of consciousness most of the time. Thankfully, because my stepfather and I waged an unholy war on each other at that point, one that had been brewing for over 20 years. I don't like being mean, but with some people you have to. Plus, I was bringing a gun to a knife fight. I didn't come by this mouth honestly.

My mom was in the hospital for over a month, receiving blood dialysis. She moved on to oral chemo to kill the poison that was circulating in her system. She ate right and started swimming since walking was too much. Ma worked hard and did everything the doctors told her, which marked a new maturity for her. She had been at death's door and didn't care to go back. Yet, we never missed a chance to remind her that this disease meant she was "one in a million!" Honestly, we never talked about it much.

Mom was not a braggart. She had the gift of gab, but always about something other than herself. Mom was a storyteller, always had been. Our Irish family lived much in the oral tradition of passing along the stories – both false and true – from elder to younger. My cousin Jocelyn and I spent many a night around my grandmother's kitchen table, listening to her sisters tell tales of the past. Their past. Our past. Our shared past. We were a close-knit family for sure. Mom had been in remission for twelve years when that angry bastard of a disease reared its God forsaken head again.

As I said earlier, it was recommended that my stepdad have surgery on his back. I guess you can call it botched surgery. His swallowing was affected. He ended up on a feeding tube. My mother, this little 4-foot-9-inch woman, was now trying to care for my 6-foot-tall stepdad. You can imagine how it went. Possibly the worst part was that he was a veteran. He had his surgery through the VA (Veterans Administration). It left a lot to be desired.

However, my stepfather made it so much harder on my mom than it had to be. He tried to eat and drink things that weren't allowed, per his doctor. That didn't stop him. He would choke, then throw up. He refused to use the walker or cane. He relied on being able to hold onto multiple objects as he walked, which is not only an outright refusal to follow the doctor's orders, but just plain demonstrating toxic masculinity at someone else's expense.

That someone else was my mother. He knew better than the professionals, and he was too much of a man's man to follow their clinical instructions. As I said, he put my mom through the ringer. So much so that the recurrence of Good Pastures came into play; this was something she had beaten before, and she told me that she thought she had "one more in me."

Yet, her condition at Christmas was scary and shocking. She, much like me, pushed through the holiday because that's what women do, but none of it was her usual over-the-top celebration. You see, we kids had always called my mom Mrs. Claus. She loved all things Christmas. Every inch of her house was decorated come Thanksgiving, and she even decked out her car in Christmas lights, candy canes, and garland. It may have been garish, but it was her. She lived her joy out loud and didn't care who heard.

Typically, soon after Halloween treats were done, she would begin holiday prep. She had a big freezer that she used to store her holiday baked goods when we were kids. It was in our creepy old basement, but we were willing to take that risk to be able to raid the cookies! This was during the Star Wars and Raiders of the Lost Ark era, so we never missed a chance to pretend we were hunting artifacts around the world or saving a planet from imminent doom. We would go down into that dank, dark basement in pairs, with a flashlight. The sugar rush of homemade Christmas cookies was an allure we were helpless to deny. Much to our chagrin, she caught on and put a padlock on the freezer. We teased her that she was being a Grinch. It didn't work.

Shortly before Christmas, I went back to my family physician. She wrote me out longer and upped the meds. I was experiencing horrible gastrointestinal issues that I will spare you the gory details of. If I am honest, they started back when my son went into crisis. I had been managing it with Imodium and Tums, ginger ale, and whatever else I could find. I called the GI doctor, and they set up testing. I did several full blood workups, an endoscopy, two stool studies, and ended up on prescription meds from them, too. My stomach was labeled "pre-ulcerous."

Alright, Kindreds, so if you have been paying attention, you can see that I was a hot mess. I had been seeing a therapist weekly for a while, and she was really helpful. She was sympathetic and gave excellent advice. She would role-play with me back when I first started seeing her. I had my reasons, but that is fodder for another book. Most of these reasons – without going totally rogue about them – are that life was freaking hard. Parenting adult children was harder. Plus, I'm not the only one who feels how changed the world is post-pandemic. Sometimes, oh, alright, many times, I have thought my mom was the lucky one. She checked out before we could, as a species, do any more harm.

Yet, we had been raised strict Irish Catholics. My siblings and I had done twelve years of Catholic school, and that is hard to shake. As enticing as lying down and never getting up again was, life had to be lived come what may.

However, we were, as my husband liked to say, "members of the C&E club." Christmas and Easter, that is. That's when we went to church. I am not going to lie; I loved the pageantry of the Catholic church. It was all I knew, until I didn't.

Over the years, I became disillusioned with the church. I had been a CCD teacher, and my children had received all of their sacraments. Yet, many negative experiences with the church led me to lean towards the agnostic mindset. Who could forget the pedophile priests'

bombshell? I mean, as Catholic school kids, we recited the jokes about priests and altar servers, but none of us believed it.

As more and more came out, I was disgusted. At the same time, Angelica was in our local Catholic kindergarten. It was suggested that she be tested for ADHD. I consented.

Back then, I had no college education. I wish I knew then what I know now. Angelica and I would have had a much healthier relationship while she was growing up if I knew then what I know now. Alas, I digress.

As kids, we were poor. Lower middle class, I guess. The library was my best friend because I couldn't afford comics and books. The library was quiet, whereas my house was always chaotic and loud. The library was warm, smelled good, and was just so peaceful. It had been my escape as a child, and in times of uncertainty, I always fall back on the old ways. I went to the library and checked out every book I could on ADHD. I educated myself. When testing was complete, it was suggested that she take meds for ADHD. That's it: no behavior chart, no time built in for extra help or decompression, nothing. I ended up pulling my daughter because it didn't take a degree to realize that she was learning absolutely nothing at this school. Nor were her fellow classmates, because she was so disruptive. (Even back then, I had a teacher's mind.) The pedophile Bishop (he was later defrocked) retorted with a nasty, vile letter telling me I was lucky he didn't lodge child abuse charges against me for refusing to medicate my child! That was just another personal riff I had with the Catholic church.

The next came the following year when Ella was to be christened. I wanted to receive Communion at her Mass, so I picked her up at the sitter's Saturday after working at the salon. We hightailed it to Confession. The priest was old, crotchety, and unknown to me. Ella had fallen asleep in her baby car seat on the way there. I carefully removed her from the car, entered the haven I loved as a child, and got in line while she slept peacefully.

When my turn came, I entered the dark confessional quietly. I set Ella's baby carrier next to me on the kneeler and began to recite the lines of old with reverence.

"Bless me, father, for I have sinned. It has been two years since my last confession, and these are my sins."

Before I could even begin to list my wrongs, he started with a raised voice: "It has been how long? And you dare to call yourself a Christian! I suppose you even received Communion without Confession all this time!" he roared.

That was all it took to wake my sleeping newborn. Ella woke with a scream and didn't stop. I was now crying too; I couldn't help it. I tried to do the "right thing" and adhere to their rules, and this is what I got? A lecture and a demeaning, patriarchal attitude? He could hear my baby crying and was still an arrogant bastard.

At this point, I was gathering my child and my purse. Between sobs, I spat back in my most indignant voice: "I most certainly did not attend Communion without a proper confession. And I have been to church during that time. But I'm not sure I will come back. You wonder why people are leaving the Church in droves? This is why!" I choked on that last word and blindly stumbled out of the confessional, still crying. Ella and I wailed our way out.

Yes, Kindreds. I carried through with the Christening the next day. Luckily, we had a young, happy priest who invited my Goddaughter up on the altar to help christen her cousin. Nevertheless, that one positive experience could not erase all the others.

Honestly, it's a wonder I dealt with the church as long as I did. The church and school we had all attended as kids refused to bury my dad when he died. Mind you, we went first through eighth grade there. Mom was super active in the school, CYO, and church. She had been for years. All in a volunteer capacity.

Yet, the priest I had known and loved as a child said "no" because my father "did not put an envelope in the collection basket each week."

Forget that mom did, and all the kids did too. He truly portrayed a particularly Christian attitude, no? The almighty buck is the only god Catholicism worships, it seems. That drove us to another church - the one my mom's parents belonged to. That was where Tony and I were married. The seeds of disillusionment had been planted way back when.

All of these experiences have led me to realize that life isn't black or white– it's all shades of gray that provide a depth, an undertone to only those who seek it. It's sort of like comics, at least the comics of my time that were black, white, and varying shades of gray. I didn't read superhero comics because even as a kid, I knew no one was coming to save us. I read Orwellian and Lovecraft-inspired comics. The sort of dark stuff that defines you, when nothing else can. Many times, I relied on my comic book knowledge as well as my Catholic learnings to help me realize that humans are inherently flawed. I love an uplifting human resource piece as much as the rest of them; heck, who doesn't want to believe in happily ever after?

Still, time and again, I watch as humans blanket the planet with harmful practices. We also have the most innate ability to hurt each other. Once more, no degree is required to see that we are the problem. What most people don't understand is that we are also the solution.

My lack of education led some to believe they could roll on me. My daughter's Catholic kindergarten was one of these. The most infuriating part is that my generation – Gen X - was raised to never speak out against the church or those who run it. This was a generational attitude, and one that allowed the pedophilia to run rampant. It was also a mindset that the boomers were trying to instill in us. They were attempting to raise us, just as many of them had been raised, to trust institutions and authority without thought or dissent. However, we were being raised for a world that had moved on. Women were going back to work, and divorce was becoming more commonplace. The Cold War was ending, and the Internet was being created. Gen X was possibly the last to begin to buy into that mindset, or our parents actually did, since we were just kids. However, Gen X was also the first generation to approach literally everything with skepticism. We invented angst, although the 90s get credit for that.

My point is that trust was placed in many of these institutions, like the church, only to have it later revealed that they betrayed that trust in the absolute worst way possible. They hid behind a collar and a theological degree. Or maybe a badge and a gun. Perhaps a title such as teacher, or coach. You get the picture, Kindreds – people, especially children, suffer so much at the hands of those they trust. It makes me want to weep. The much criticized, rarely lauded Gen X were the first to actually defy these institutions with any success. All because the general public felt degrees, awards, accolades and the like were a reason to trust. In my experience, there is far too much value placed on these things. Or maybe it's my Gen X showing – I trust no one anymore.

As I have alluded to before, Gen X grew up in a world that no longer exists. We saw and did things that would have The Woke in a tizzy. This is probably as good a time as any to remark that I am an Independent. I do not have much in common with our two mainstream parties. I see very little value in what they both spout, which is opposite ends of the spectrum. I am proud to be the outsider looking in. It's a role I have relished much of my life. I have never minded being alone. I guess that's because I get so little of it.

While we are strolling down memory lane, might I mention that I often wonder whatever happened to good old-fashioned work, humility, and loyalty taking you places? I fully realize that makes me sound old, but it's true, and while you're at – get off my lawn!

So, what then is the point of all this? I ask myself that on the daily, my Kindreds. I guess it's that life is seriously, ridiculously hard. Many times it doesn't have to be. It simply is because of the decisions we or those we are attached to make. You know, free will and all that. Yet, there are times when we all feel like the higher power has it in for us as if the universe is giving us double middle digits. That's why self-care is so necessary. It's also so elusive, though.

Maybe your self-care looks like jogging a mile before work. Or, it's taking a long shower in the morning. For others, it is reading their phone while having tea, coffee, or breakfast (I wish I could say "reading their newspaper," but let's be real.)

During these dark days, self-care for me was just making it through the day. I no longer planned in advance, and I wasn't working. I didn't watch the news, I didn't keep in touch with anyone, and I didn't take care of my family like I typically would.

In fact, my family orbited their own personal hell. My oldest, with the baby, was trapped in a violent relationship with the daddy. My son spiraled in and out of crisis. My mom was ill, but making small gains. My stepfather was still a walking corpse. My poor husband was the sole breadwinner and was trying to wrap his head around all of it. And I kept on keeping on in my own injured way.

Chapter 4

The New Year brought nothing new. We were all in a holding pattern of pain, just waiting for the next shoe to drop. With this many negatives going on in one family, it was only a matter of time. Not a single one of us was coping well with life's curve balls, and we fluttered between waking and sleeping.

That is to say, we were not always aware when awake, and we were not always resting when sleeping. I personally flitted between catatonic and barely moving. I continued therapy and doctor's appointments – both family and GI. I underwent another battery of tests with the GI. I continued to have panic attacks, but they were becoming more infrequent. Still, I couldn't make decisions, my sleep cycles were screwed up, my body ached, and I felt like my head was full of cotton. All this in addition to almost constant nausea and diarrhea. The testing showed nothing abnormal. I was put on different meds. I continued to see my family practitioner – Lena – but I lost a lot of hours. I honestly couldn't account for much of the time after that first panic attack. I no longer knew the day of the week. Makeup and nice hair were no longer a possibility, because it was a good day if I showered. I self -medicated with alcohol. That was my self-care. I know it's not the healthiest of ways to cope, but it was the only thing keeping me semi-sane.

Things began to settle in my family. My mom was getting Procrit shots that helped stimulate her kidneys. She was very bloated with fluid, and this was sure to help, as it did last time. My kids were holding their own. I was still attending weekly therapy sessions, in addition to my meds. I was doing everything I had to do on the work end - sending doctors' notes and updates, while also asking honest questions. That same HR department that didn't post vacancies didn't even bother to answer me when I reached out with these updates and questions. It was infuriating that while they ignored my pleas for help, they continued to send out self-care emails, such as the "Weigh in Weekly" one.

While we remained perpetually short-staffed and while teachers were losing their prep periods, HR wanted us to participate in a weight loss challenge. How absolutely out of touch they were with our needs. The fact that their ignorance was willing and calculated is beyond my comprehension. Wouldn't it be easier just to do your job?

Due to all of this, I relied heavily on Liz and my vice principal for information and guidance, because my principal was equally as useless as the HR director. My principal's idea of educational leadership was walking around the building, talking to people about beer and sports. He never chipped in, nor did he help out when we were critically understaffed.

In fact, the vice principal did most of the work because my principal was seriously inept. It's unreal how many people are awful at their job yet still hold onto it. Furthermore, my district is notorious for promoting individuals who have no business being in administration. I wonder if it ever occurred to anyone that this was a huge part of their problem?

Anyhow, I returned to my family practitioner, Lena, and she wrote me back into school. The way I looked at it, I was about as whole as I was going to get this school year. If things could just stay copacetic at home, I could pull it off. My psyche was set up so that if things were not tight at home, I needed them tight at work, and vice versa. When nothing is tight, to quote Achebe, "the center doesn't hold." (If you have never read this author, do yourself a favor and check him out.)

I was poised to return on a Wednesday. That gave me about ten days to get myself situated. Then I got the call that my mom tested positive for COVID-19. My step father had been going to therapy to try to get stronger. He picked it up there and brought it home to her. Now she couldn't attend her doctor's appointments to receive her Procrit shots. These shots were starting her down the path to recovery again, but once Covid grasped onto her, it wouldn't let go.

She had been hesitant about going to the hospital because she still had unpaid bills from her stay when it was discovered that the Good Pastures was back. We urged her to go. She wouldn't.

"I'll be alright" was her standard reply.

It is absolutely worth noting that a 73-year-old woman who had worked her entire life was delaying care due to fear of medical bills. Yes, she had Medicaid and whatever other plan was offered to her. None of it was enough – the deductibles were huge. I told her we would work out a payment plan, not to sweat it. I just wanted her to concentrate on getting better.

As the days wore on, though, she was getting sicker and just kept testing positive. It hurt her swollen hands to text, and she coughed the whole time she talked on the phone, making it really hard to communicate with her. I had stayed away because I babysat Kaleb and was terrified, I could pass Covid to him. I would drop off groceries on her porch every weekend when I was up in the mountains.

My stepfather found her the next Sunday morning, and she was barely conscious. Even then, she was not agreeable to going to the hospital. However, in her weakened state, we were able to get her there. She was admitted and immediately put on oxygen. Good Pastures can affect your kidneys, causing fluid to build up in the body. This is mostly waste that your kidneys can not evacuate. When fluid builds up that much and your body can not rid itself, your lungs are next on the list.

Last time my mom battled the beast, she was given oral chemo to help with the toxins that were circulating in her system. She was too weak for that this time around.

Furthermore, it also affects your heart, and COVID has been known to do the same. Overcoming this particular viral cocktail paired with her pre-existing condition was an insurmountable task. Regardless, if anyone could beat it, it was my mom.

For the first week she was there, we tried to text and call. As the days wore on, though, she grew weaker and weaker. Her arms were a bloody mess because they couldn't keep her veins from collapsing. She wasn't eating. I wished upon all the stars in the universe that I could go in and see her. However, the risk to my baby grandson was too great. I ended up having to rely on my stepfather for information, because they let him in with a mask and gown.

Even though this weighed heavily on my mind, I just always assumed she would beat it. She had made an amazing recovery the first time she had Good Pastures, but now, with the added load of Covid, the situation was downright frightful. However, if you knew my mom, you would know what a fighter she was. She still had plenty of living and loving left to do. Heck, we had just been blessed with her first great-grandchild. She was in love with Kaleb, and I knew he was a huge motivation for her to pull through. It had never entered my mind that she wouldn't make it. She was the strongest woman I know. To me, it was a no-brainer. Mom would do what she always did – fight through.

That weekend was a long one Monday was Presidents' Day. My hubs and I headed to our little cabin in the Poconos. We had bought it with our retirement money and paid a hefty fine for early withdrawal, but it was our Zen spot. It was tiny, so not much to clean and maintain. Plus, it was quiet. Delaware County (Delco), where I live, is becoming too much like Philadelphia. Don't get me wrong, I bleed Eagles green, live for the Phillies, and pray for the Flyers. I just do it from the relative comfort of my couch.

Anyhow, my mom was still in the hospital up there. She had bought a little place about five to ten minutes from us. Her sister lived about 15 minutes down the mountain from us. (That was Jocelyn's mother.) My mom had always been a New Jersey shore retiree – opting to spend winters in a tiny trailer in New Port Richey, Florida. She sold the Jersey place and got the little mountain house. This was perfect for Mom, with her sister & I so close by most weekends.

This situation was still a conundrum for me. I wanted to see my mom so badly, but I was terrified of what might happen if I did. Kaleb was a pandemic baby. He hadn't been anywhere much other than my house and the occasional appointment. We had, as a family, not gone to concerts or over-crowded venues as a rule. He literally had no exposure to nasty viruses and colds, so he didn't have any natural immunity other than breast milk. COVID-19 vaccines were not made for children his age.

Additionally, I was back in the building just three days later and already had a sore throat. Schools are teeming with germs, and when the classrooms aren't cleaned on the regular, well, you get the idea. I was not risking bringing my ma anything else to fight off.

As I said, I relied on my step father for information. My aunt had braved going in, and she didn't have much to share. My mom was hooked up to a multitude of machines, and it was difficult to communicate with all the beeps, whirs, and whooshes. Add in the masks that everyone was wearing, and it was almost impossible to communicate effectively.

When I spoke with my step father that weekend, he told me that her veins kept collapsing, and they couldn't get an IV into her. He said her arms were such a mess from all of the needles that the skin was breaking down. He said that she is in and out of consciousness and other than that, there wasn't much to report. Mom had texted me once that week about her arms. That was the last text I ever received from her.

Heading home Sunday night, I was cruising when my step dad called, crying and screaming. I pulled over because I couldn't understand what he was saying. I finally realized he was telling me the hospital called, and Mom had crashed. They revived her more than once and put her on a vent. The doctors suggested we arrive as soon as possible. I turned the car around and headed back. I called my husband and my aunt, the only one left in my mom's family. I arranged to meet my husband and pick up my aunt. I prayed the whole way there. I begged God not to take her while we were racing to the hospital in Scranton.

As we walked up to the hospital, we noticed my mom's car out front, all smashed up. We looked at it, uncomprehending. I think we were in the beginning stages of shock. At the nurse's station, we gave my mother's name and they ushered us up to the ICU. She was in a room enclosed in glass, so everything was visible. She was in the bed, intubated and unconscious.

We were allowed to go in, one at a time. We had to put on gloves, a mask, and a gown. I went first. I still felt like I was coming down with something, so I didn't dare kiss her. In my mind, she was beating this and didn't need another thing to fight off. So, I just stroked her hair, talking quietly to her.

All of the experts seem to agree that unconscious people can still hear what is being said to them. I told my mom how much we loved her and how she was the glue in our family; we needed her. I reminded her that we finally had a new baby in the family to enjoy, and that she, I, and Kaleb had big plans for next summer.

Conversely, the experts also say that you should give your loved one permission to let go if they are suffering. It was very obvious that my mom was. She was bloated beyond recognition, and there was blood crusted all around her mouth and neck. Her arms were black and purple and covered in clear bandages. Under them, her arms were raw and bleeding. There wasn't much skin left on them. She resembled a burn victim. My heart broke looking at her. I didn't want her to hear me cry, so I gave little hysterical laughs that sounded more like a bark than anything else. I was very close to breaking down.

Finally, I told her that "none of us want to say goodbye, but if you can't fight anymore, it's ok to let go."

With that, the doctor came in and said her latest test showed the vent wasn't positioned correctly, so I had to leave the room while they repositioned it.

Both my aunt and husband took their turns with my mom. While they did, the doctor who had been fixing her vent told me that she has a particularly nasty strain of Covid and we should be careful who we are around until we are certain we didn't catch it. He added, "If your mom makes it through the night, she has a very good chance of beating this."

That, of course, just cemented it in my mind that she was going to pull through. He ended the conversation by telling me he had been checking my step dad's blood sugar (he is diabetic), and we really needed to get him home and make him eat and rest. It was a tall task getting him to agree to leave, but finally we did. Both he and I kept looking over our shoulders at my mom lying in that bed as we walked away.

Had I known then what I do now, I never would have left. I would have stayed and held her hand all night, because little did, I realize the bronchitis I was developing wouldn't make a shred of difference in the end.

There was still the small issue of my mom's car sitting out front, all crashed up. "What happened?" I asked my step father.

He replied that he was so upset driving here that he crashed into a curb and a stop sign. Tony pulled the car into the hospital parking lot so it wouldn't be on the street. Pieces of it were falling off as the car limped its way into the parking space. He gathered them up and threw them in the trunk.

It was a long ride back to the mountain. None of us spoke much. We dropped my step dad and aunt off, and crawled into bed sometime after 2 a.m. By 4 am, my step father was calling and crying. He wanted to go back to the hospital. I got up, went into the bathroom, and promptly started throwing up. My head was pounding, and every part of my body ached. The room was spinning. I went in and woke my husband.

"I can't drive," I said, crying.

Tony is a rock in times of crisis, but even he was at his wits' end. He sleepily got up and put on pants. He told me to go back to bed. I did.

When he returned, I must have been sleeping like the dead, because I never even heard him. I slept until 7 am when my aunt called. She was heading back to the hospital and wanted me to come. I told her how sick I felt and that I couldn't even drive my step dad there. I told her to call me when she gets there. The next time my phone rang was at 8:20 am. It was my aunt calling to tell me Mom was gone. I don't remember how I responded. I just remember standing in the living room crying.

Possibly the hardest thing I have ever had to do was tell my kids that their Grandma was gone. I wanted to pack up and head home to tell them in person. Tony warned me off that idea, "Not in the age of social media, Jen." He said.

He was afraid someone would post something about it, and he was right. I started with Angelica. I told her I had some bad news. When I actually said the words "Grandma passed this morning," she was in shock. She asked me to repeat myself, and I did. The howl of pain she let out when it hit her is a sound I will never forget. I stayed on the phone with her, trying to provide some comfort. While on the phone, Ella started calling Angelica. "Mom, I can't talk to her," she wailed. I agreed to hang up and call.

Unfortunately, Ella had seen a post from a family member who didn't realize not everyone knew about my mom's passing. She wanted to know if it was true and what happened. I felt my heart splinter a little more each time I said it. I explained that Grandma had taken a turn for the worse last night and was put on a ventilator. I told her she crashed many times and they revived her, but her lungs collapsed and her kidneys started shutting down. I wished I were with my kids delivering this horrible news with a hug.

Lastly, I had to tell Aaron. I was seriously worried about what the news would do to him. I woke him up, so I could tell he was utterly confused on top of being heartbroken. My mom was extremely close to my kids. I told him I was coming home and to meet me at the house.

Tony and I gathered our things in silence. Just like my ride to the mountains the night the student attempted to charge me, I recall nothing of the ride home. I stopped and checked on my step father before leaving. He was devastated. We all were. I don't really remember arriving home either. I do know that my brother and my adult children were there. At some point, Jocelyn's two adult daughters, Kellie and Melanie, came over. They were super tight with my mom, too. We all sat around drinking and crying. Eventually, I went to bed.

My step dad was retrieved by his kids, who live in New York. It had been decided that my step brother, whom I haven't seen in like twenty years, was driving my step dad down to the funeral home in Delco to make the final arrangements. My aunt and I were meeting them there. It was the same funeral home we had used to bury my father, my grandfather, my nan, and Jocelyn's husband. Some tradition, huh?

We arrived first and went in to wait. The funeral parlor was frozen in time. It had that timeless décor that never went out of style. Yet, I was still amazed that everything looked just how it had when I was first here 32 years ago to bury my dad. The funeral director and I had gone to grade school together. That is just how Delco was. You knew someone everywhere you went. That wasn't always a good thing; however, in this instance, it was. As he ushered us into his office, my step father called to say he was almost there.

When he got to the funeral home, his son was helping him walk. He was an absolute mess. He couldn't hold a pen to sign the paperwork, he couldn't form a sentence without crying, and in the end, I made most of the decisions because he simply couldn't.

This left very little down time for grief, and that was a good thing, because once I let the floodgates open, they didn't close. Every morning, for months, Mom was the first thing I thought about when I opened my eyes. The prospect of going the rest of my life without ever seeing or talking to her again hurt beyond words.

Even so, I did what I always do. I put on my big girl panties and took care of business. If I kept busy, I could do that. Avoidance is a coping mechanism that I use often, usually to my own detriment. Old dogs and new tricks, my Kindreds. We are all familiar with that adage.

My Mom's body was in Scranton. She needed to be transported to Delaware County for her burial. She wasn't there the day we went to the funeral home to plan her services. As such, we ended up making her funeral for the Monday after she died, which was exactly one week from when she passed away. My school district gave three days of bereavement leave for a parent. That wasn't even long enough for her body to be brought to the funeral home, let alone notify everyone, write and post the obituary, plan the funeral, and have the services. My body reacted to this new level of stress the same way it had been: I was back to throwing up everything I ate, and if it didn't come out that end, it came out the other.

Once again, I relied on alcohol to get me through the days and nights. At least I didn't throw it up, was the way I looked at it. Plus, wine counts as a fruit, right?

Being the eldest, it fell to me to do most of everything. My aunt chose and paid for the flowers. I was grateful, but also felt terrible for her. Mom was the only family she had left. She had chosen pink flowers, so I found a pink dress to compliment to. The funeral director warned me that her arms were an absolute mess and she would require long sleeves. Do you have any idea how difficult it is to find a woman's dress with sleeves, my Kindreds? Even in the dead of winter! Alas, another book topic for another day is the ridiculous standards of women's dress in our modern-day society. Once again, I digress.

My mom's husband and I were in constant contact that week. He went back and forth on what he wanted and didn't want. I agreed, then did what I knew my mother would want. I called everyone she was close with. I explained to her for the hundredth time what had happened. It was incredibly difficult to get through these conversations without breaking down. I tried to have a drop of dignity, though. As an English undergraduate, writing was my passion, so I personally penned my mother's obituary. I included exactly what I thought should be in there. I made it funny and sweet – just like my mom.

My girls created a video tribute featuring pictures of my mother, friends, and family at various functions, vacations, birthdays, and holidays over the years. We carefully chose the pictures to be included and set the video to Fleetwood Mac tunes – Mom's favorite band. It was a beautiful way to honor an amazing woman. We were fortunate enough to have fantastic friends who sent meals to us that week. (Thanks, Jersey, Carolina, and the New York crew!) I invited what was left of the family to dinner, and everyone brought pictures of Mom. We ate, cried, reminisced, and made gorgeous picture boards for the funeral. Angelica has always been a very talented artist, and she drew beach scenes: oceans, crabs, palm trees, fish, and sea shells. All things near and dear to her grandmother.

As the funeral approached, I checked off all the tedious little boxes that nobody ever thinks of until a loved one dies. My step-dad requested slippers instead of shoes, since my mom's feet hurt all the time. The funeral director said her undergarments have to be new.

"Who knew you had to be buried in brand new underwear?" I muttered to myself while stumbling through Kohl's department store. With jewelry, nail polish, and even stockings – who could be comfortable in that for eternity? I made a mental note to myself to be cremated.

As always, sleep was elusive no matter how weary I was. It was early in the morning, two days before my mom's funeral, and I was finally asleep. Aaron came running into my bedroom, yelling. I was concerned about him. He had that wild look in his eyes that typically signaled an oncoming mental crisis. Thrusting the phone at me, I hold it up to my ear. All I can hear is Ella weeping. She was trying to talk, but it didn't make sense. I leapt out of bed and held a finger in my ear to try to decipher what she was saying.

I finally yelled, "Ella! I cannot understand! You have to calm down."

She had been t-boned right around the corner. Her car was totaled. I hung up and ran downstairs to go get her. In the driveway, the sunlight hit my face, and everything swayed, myself included. Then the vomit came. I can't remember the last time I had eaten, and as I bent over retching, green liquid sprayed out of my mouth like a fountain. It reminded me of the crappy Kool-Aid we drank as unsuspecting kids.

"What even is that?" I thought in a dreaming sort of way. I started to see black dots and hear a buzzing sound. I knew I was going to pass out. I tried to grab the bumper of my vehicle. My bladder chose that moment to let go, and that roused me. I duck -walked back into the house to tell Tony that he was next up on the chaos coaster. Shortly after, Ella arrived home, sore, bruised, and crying. I had changed and cleaned up. She allowed me to envelop her in a big, Momma-bear hug. Crying, she clung to me.

"Why does life suck so bad anymore, Mom?" She got out in between sobs.

For that, I had no answer. My mind may have been broken, but I knew enough to get a doctor's appointment before the funeral. I didn't want to be coughing my way through her services.

Another reason I like our practice is that they are really good about getting you in quickly for sick visits. I assumed, incorrectly, that I would have Lena. When Dr. Lowes walked into the room, I was surprised. He didn't look anything like I had expected him to. He was short and thin. He had graying hair and wore large, round eyeglasses. I am unsure what I expected him to look like, actually. I just didn't picture someone diminutive.

He introduced himself and told me I could lower my mask. For this, I was thankful, because my ears hurt too much to put my hearing aids in. (I blame all the rock concerts I've attended over the years.) I had broken down and visited an audiologist the previous summer. It is remarkable how much I have come to rely on reading lips. Dr. Lowes pulled his mask down too and introduced himself. He even shook my hand, which is rare in the Covid world.

He pulled up my medical history on the computer and reviewed it while asking me what had brought me in. I explained that I had swollen glands, sore throat, blocked ears and head, plus a burning cough. Lowes looked me over, doing all the light shining and throat-probing stuff. He told me I had an acute upper respiratory infection that turned into bronchitis and a double ear infection.

This was the umpteenth time I had contracted this in the past decade. I used to be so healthy. My kids would ask when sick: "Why don't you get sick, Mom? You are the one taking care of us."

I always answered, full of fledgling hope: "Because God knows Mommies need to stay well."

While Lowes was sending prescriptions electronically to the pharmacy, he made small talk and asked what I had done over the long President's weekend. I couldn't help it. I blurted out, "Well, my mom died on Monday, so …." I trailed off.

Dr. Lowes whipped around in his chair. His eyes were even larger than his glasses made them seem. "Your mom died on Monday? My mom died Monday!"

Of course, I was all like, "No way!"

Suddenly, we were in a club together. He asked how she passed, and I gave him the abbreviated version. He looked so sad, I reciprocated and let my guard down for a minute or two.

"How old was she?" he inquired.

"73," I answered. In the next breath, I asked about his mom.

"She was elderly, 92 years old. But that doesn't make it any easier." He replied. "I started my morning every day with a phone call to her. I will miss her so much."

We both got teary-eyed. He stood, and I followed suit.

When I extended my hand to shake again, he pulled me into a big bear hug. He was surprisingly strong for one so slight. I hugged him back, and he assured me my scripts would be ready to pick up.

"Take care of yourself," he called as I headed out. I turned and gave him the thumbs up and headed to my car.

Even though we had just met, I felt a kinship with this man. He was most definitely a Kindred, I thought to myself. Driving to the pharmacy, I reflected on the situation further. Sometimes people are put in your path at just the right time. I don't know if it was God, the Universe, or some higher power. All I knew was that I didn't feel so alone that afternoon.

Chapter 5

In my world, it is an irrefutable law that when the Universe decides to screw with me, she is damn thorough. I was the living, breathing version of Murphy's Law, which, according to the Cambridge Dictionary, is: "the principle that if it is possible for something to go wrong, it will go wrong."

I did my best to limit the damage that could occur, but life often goes off script. Aaron got a lift home and opted not to spend the night at my house before the funeral. He looked like a caged animal that was eager to escape. I was too bone weary even to attempt to talk him out of being alone. He was having hallucinations again – a symptom of his schizophrenia.

When Aaron spirals down into crisis, he always thinks his Dad and I are out to get him. His hallucinations were replete with audio, meaning he heard voices. These were always super negative and uber persistent. All I could do was pray he would make the funeral the next day since he was a pallbearer.

We arrived at the church early the following morning. I reached into my purse to make sure I had my eulogy tucked away. We carried in the photo boards and handed them off to the funeral parlor people to set up. I also had my mom's press awards to showcase. She was a reporter until she retired.

As I made my way down the aisle towards my mom's casket, the priest came out and grabbed me. He was Middle Eastern, with a thick accent. Even with my hearing aids in, I struggled to understand him. He led me back behind the altar. I looked around, remembering how excited I was as a child to be back here, in this secret spot. My mom had always signed me up for the Easter procession that was held every year at my childhood parish. We would gather behind the altar beforehand.

Yet, there was no joy this time. I was irritated to have not been given the courtesy of viewing my mother's body before being preyed upon. He wanted to pump me for information about my mom for his sermon.

"Seriously?" I thought. No preparation.

My ma apparently wasn't important enough in his eyes to warrant a phone call to ask these questions that he was now pummeling me with. I answered to the best of my ability, given I was simmering. I did not want to get my Irish up at Mom's funeral. That's what the luncheon was for. I am kidding, Kindreds. Well, sort of. He looked over my eulogy and took a pen. He proceeded to cross out huge pieces while I watched in dismay. Turning to me, he said, "This is too much. What will I talk about?" He ended with a chuckle.

It was like being held prisoner by my own manners. The priest continued to ask more questions. Even with my hearing aids in, his accent was too difficult to understand. I glanced at the clock. It was 9:20. The viewing was set to open to the public in just ten minutes! I had gotten there early to lay eyes on her and make absolutely certain everything looked as it should. This priest – I mean, this putz – was cutting into that precious time deeply.

"Excuse me, Father," I cut him off. "I would like to go view my mother's body before people arrive."

I didn't wait for an answer. I simply walked away and out the door to the altar. I didn't bother bowing when I walked past the altar to the casket. I knelt down on the velvet kneeler and looked her over. The dress was beautiful on her. It was the exact shade of rose as the flowers.

Speaking of which, my aunt out did herself. The arrangements towered on either side and dwindled down to smaller ones. My Mom loved flowers and was an avid gardener, so this was perfect. The casket was fit for royalty. Her face was so puffy, though. Like she had been crying for days. My heart twisted in my chest as I knelt before her.

This was Mom lying here. The same one who saw me through every illness, obstacle, and milestone, who was my biggest cheerleader. Mom that baked, cooked, and made amazing mixed drinks. Mom the most genuine, kind-hearted person with a sarcastic, smug sense of humor. Mom - the very best Grandmother a kid could ask for. Mom who I would do anything for, and who would do anything for me.

"There is no bond like it," I thought sadly.

I forced myself to gaze upon her as long as I could, knowing full well this was the last time I would lay eyes on her. I felt the tears beginning to well up, and I pushed them down. I was well medicated and therefore prepared. I had a eulogy to get through.

My step-dad arrived and was worse than he had been at the funeral home. He couldn't walk at all. His grown sons were literally dragging him down the church aisle. One was on each side of him, hefting him up, under his arm. The tips of his highly polished dress shoes dragged on the carpet as they pulled him along. He was blubbering, crying, and not making much sense. I left him alone at the casket and went to the back of the church to make sure everything was in place.

The video my girls had made was playing, and on a table to the right were all her press awards from a journalistic career that spanned decades. The picture boards were lined up down the aisle for people to peruse while waiting to pay their respects.

When mourners began to arrive, the boys dragged my step-father to the first pew and he set up shop there. He was shaking, but very quiet- just staring at his wife lying in repose. I wondered, and not for the first time, if he would make it through the day.

As guests filed in to pay their respects, I took the lead. I stood at the front receiving people, giving hugs, and thanking them for coming. There was a pretty good turnout, considering my Mom only had one sister and a few cousins left.

It became time to wheel the casket into the back of the church for our private final goodbyes before the Mass began. Tony and my oldest step-brother were dragging my step-dad to the back of the church. He was crying and trying to get his legs to work. I was walking backwards, coaxing him towards the coffin. I grabbed a chair and set him up in front of the casket. It was so hard to watch. Here I was, waiting to give my mom her last kiss goodbye, when Ella came back looking anxious.

"Mom, the priest is looking for you. He thought I was you, and he is mad."

I sighed and gave my Mom a kiss on the head. Even though it wasn't my first time touching a dead body, I was shocked when I felt the skull under her hair. My mother was very short – 4 '9 or thereabouts at the time of her death – and I regularly kissed her on the head since she was so tiny. This was nothing like that. All of the fluid and warmth had gone from her. I stifled a sob and turned away to put out yet another fire. I walked down the aisle with my head down, fighting against the tears that were burning the back of my eyes.

"I told you to start your eulogy at 10," he said angrily, pointing at the clock.

It was now 10:10.

"Father, the body isn't even in the church right now!" I whispered vehemently.

His eyes grew large. "Where is it?" he asked.

"We were in the back saying goodbye and closing the casket!" I hissed.

He made a shooing motion, and I went and sat in the front row next to Tony. Aaron had finally shown up, looking disheveled and trapped. He refused to sit with us and instead lingered around a few rows back.

Once the casket was in place, the lid sealed shut, I went up to the lectern to deliver my eulogy. I glanced down at the speech that I had so lovingly and painstakingly penned. It now had scribbles and large sections crossed out. I did the best I could to piece it back together without taking too much time. It always seems to come down to that, doesn't it? We simply never have enough time.

After I finished, Mass began. When the priest got up to deliver his sermon, he was incomprehensible. Not only was his accent so thick it was difficult to understand him, but he kept ranting about the bread my Mom would make and the fish she loved to catch. I get that he was attempting to tie fish and loaves in, but he missed the mark entirely.

While I sat there listening to his gibberish, I began to grow angry. "My mother deserved a better sermon than this clown can deliver," I thought.

This was followed by another – that Mom would think this was hilarious! She had an incredible sense of humor, and the irony of this did not escape me. I pictured her ghost in church listening to the barrage of drivel coming from this "Man of God's" mouth. I stifled a giggle and gave Tony a side glance. He caught it and made a face of genuine distaste. I know how he felt. The bum, I mean priest, didn't even bother to attend the graveside service. He sent a nun in his place. Even now, the Catholic church wonders why people are rejecting it. I was hurt that the priest didn't think this was important enough to show up for. Honestly, though, I was more shocked that he wasn't going to tag along to the luncheon for a free meal!

We held the funeral luncheon at the same restaurant we had used for the funerals of every family member, because of tradition. It was nice and sad all at the same time.

Once again, my son refused to sit with us. In fact, he ended up trying to fistfight my mom's old neighbor, because Aaron thought the guy was talking about him. This man is in his 60's. Angelica's boyfriend dragged Aaron out.

Meanwhile, I went from table to table, saying all the right things. I had a drink in my hand the entire time. Alcohol was my preferred coping mechanism, but I believe I have mentioned that before. That night at home, I drank myself into a stupor and stumbled to bed. This wouldn't be so bad if I actually could stay asleep, but I hadn't had a full night's sleep in I couldn't tell you how long. The dark, sleepless hours in the dead of the night were not my friend. The memories and thoughts that ran through my head were just as black as the sky above me.

Chapter 6

In the days that followed, I sank deeper into depression. The only parent I had left was gone. The only person who knew me inside and out was no longer alive. I was an orphan.

That Wednesday, I went back to work. I had missed over a week to bury my mom. I hoped that the students would be kind. I made my way to the classroom I would be subbing in for the remainder of the year. I promised myself not to be bitter and just make the best of it.

"The three days I spent with them before Mom died went pretty well," I muttered to myself as I switched the light on.

My eyes could not believe what I was seeing. I was frozen to the spot, staring and blinking, uncomprehending what I was looking at. The chalkboard, which was covered in whiteboard paper (we are a high-poverty district, remember), was now covered in curse words written in marker. The white board itself was carved up with some sort of sharp instrument. I went to the teacher's desk to grab my board cleaner solution and eraser. Both were gone.

It was at that point that I noticed someone had written graffiti on the teacher's desk.

I couldn't figure out what it said, so I walked over to the windows to raise the shade. When I did, I found that the windows were smashed and wouldn't close or lock. Below the broken windows were radiators with more graffiti scrawled on them. I started to cry. I just couldn't help it.

Bewildered, I looked around as the tears flowed. There was trash everywhere. Desks were askew, and textbooks littered the floor. Broken markers, pens, pencils - most likely mine - were scattered throughout the room on every surface.

Again, I hunted for an Expo eraser and couldn't find one. My teacher 's supplies and prize box, which I had used to encourage students to follow expectations, were ransacked. Now I was openly sobbing. I called the office and waited for the cleaning lady. Doll was sweet and super helpful. When she walked in, she let out a visible gasp. "What the hell happened?" she asked.

"I don't know," I blubbered.

She came over to me and enveloped me in a big hug. This made me cry even harder.

"Don't be nice to me or mean to me," I thought crazily. "Just let me be the ghost I want to be," I almost said.

There was precious little time before the first bell rang. Doll helped me clean up and marveled that someone had also burned the board in spots.

"Great. So they had a knife and a lighter?" I asked the air, the universe, and myself.

I turned to her. "How did no one get hurt?" I asked.

"Mr. McDickell is lucky no one did," she answered.

"True story," I thought. The bell rang, and I tried to pull myself together.

"Need anything?" she asked.

"Something to write with," I replied, thinking of the Old Van Halen song. This cheered me, and I went to let the students in. They surged through the door, pushing each other and yelling. I tried in vain to quiet them down.

Eventually, I did, or at least as quiet as they were ever going to get. I filled students in on where I had been and why. A few offered their condolences, but most ignored me. I sent students to their lockers row by row and attempted to take lunch orders. This took much longer than it should have, as many students remained talking, wandering, and shoving.

This was big in middle school. Students could not seem to keep their hands to themselves. One girl in particular, whom I will call Jaylen, was the captain of chaos. She was very big for her age and had a voice to match. She could be heard over anyone else, and this pleased her.

As I wandered around taking lunch orders, she kept screaming, "Dead. I'm dead," and staring at me. I think she was trying to get to me, and I refused to let her have the pleasure. I ignored her and carried on. We got through the homeroom period, and then it was time to change classes.

As the students filed out, some new ones pushed their way in. I tried to maintain the peace as students came in. Many people sat in the wrong seats, making the seating chart useless. As I tried to take roll, the trouble makers kept laughing at me because I was calling people by the wrong names.

With most students sitting in the wrong seats, it was difficult to get it right. I decided to pick and choose my battles and let them sit where they wanted. While I was showing the video of the day, a handful of students continued to be disruptive. It was surely a shame for those who wanted to watch the video and participate in the group discussion afterwards. Again and again, I implored them to hush and be quiet. All to no avail. I was nearing my wits' end when a few shoving matches broke out.

All of a sudden, it was hard to breathe. We were still wearing masks in school, and that didn't help. The room started to spin. I started yelling, but didn't remember what I was saying. Thankfully, the ESL teacher came in to take her groups. She told me to go get myself together.

Out in the hallway, I was no better. I bent over, taking deep, whooshing breaths.

"No," I thought, "this isn't happening."

I stumbled down the hallway to the principal's office. I went in crying and not really making sense. I muttered something about resigning and told him he needed to send someone down to that classroom immediately, as I was leaving. I was in the midst of another panic attack, and I said the wrong thing. Who could blame me? I went back to the classroom to gather my things. I was taking giant breaths that made noises under my mask. I continued to rant about how this was all impossible. Everything was impossible. Why did I think I could do this? I waited for relief to come. It never did. Here I was having a panic attack, yelling at students, and Mr. McDickell still couldn't be bothered being a leader and sending someone down to relieve me.

This infuriated me even more, and I called the office to ask where my relief was. Looking back, I think I thought I was talking, but being so totally freaked out, I am unsure what even transpired. I couldn't hear myself, just that buzzing that I had previously heard when I lost my shit. I tried to yell above it. The ESL teacher told me just to go. She would watch the students until someone came. I wheeled my ransacked cart out of the room and made my way down the hall to my old classroom to drop off the cart. The vice principal, whom I really liked, met me. He followed me to my room. I pushed the door open and walked in.

Everything was moved around, and fans were set up. I looked down at the floor. It flooded sometimes during heavy rain, but there was no rainwater. I squinted my eyes to try to figure out what was all over the floor. Then the smell hit me. It was sewage! Raw sewage just caked the floor of my classroom.

"Sorry about all this," my vice principal said.

I ignored him and continued to sob, gathering my things.

"Is there anything I can do for you?" he asked gently.

I just shook my head "no," and hustled my way out.

Once in the car, I texted my principal and let him know I meant to take disability and not resign. In my panic, I said something wrong.

"Ok, no problem," he responded.

I drove home crying and wheezing. When I arrived, I immediately took an emergency medication and powered up my laptop to see what was going on. There was an email from the head of HR stating that he was aware of what had transpired and was concerned, as this was my first day back.

"You're concerned?" I screamed at my computer. What a joke!

He went on to say that I should "reflect" on what had taken place, while he would do the same, and he would let me know when they had decided on, if any, disciplinary consequences.

Before I could even think, I fired back a response saying something to the effect that this was entirely his fault for not posting openings in a timely fashion. I went on to emphasize that this would have never happened if I were doing just my job, which I was hired for seven years ago. However, his failure to do his job trickled down to me time and time again.

It was then that I saw a message from McDickell, the principal.

"Had to let HR know you resigned."

Had to let them know? I told him I was not resigning, and he said, 'No problem.'

This loser was throwing me under the bus to preserve his dumb ass! I mean, when it was discovered that the classroom was completely trashed and he had let it happen, he knew it wouldn't be good.

"So go with the flow and make me look crazy?" I seriously pinched myself. Was this a bad dream?

Our kids had graduated together, and he lived near me. How could he do that? Especially after all the unpaid hours I put in for PBIS and other programs. I was now fuming as well as jumping out of my skin with anxiety.

Of course, I sent a reply to him, too. I told him that the classroom was trashed, and he let it happen on his watch. I detailed that weapons and a lighter were involved. I highlighted how unsafe this was, especially considering there were open, broken windows all weekend, through which anyone could have gained entrance to the school.

"No employee should have to walk into this, let alone a struggling employee who just buried her mother!" I ended the email.

"How in the hell had I come to this?" I wondered aloud. Any hope I had that life would get better was now gone. "How will I pay my bills?" I wailed. I put my head down to cry.

Over the course of the next few days, I tried to get anyone to listen to me. My inner circle was sympathetic and supportive. My school district was anything but that, and as for my union, they were particularly ineffective.

Which may shock some. The news media portrays teachers as these ruthless creatures who are protected by this powerful, formidable union. If you watch television at all, you have likely seen images of teachers and union leaders picketing and pushing for better working conditions. They have crafty signs and matching T-shirts. They stand arm in arm, the figure of solidarity.

This was especially prevalent during the return to learning from the pandemic. We were portrayed as the enemy, and the unions representing teachers were equally despised. Everyone knows that education unions, such as the PSEA, pump money into political campaigns. They literally send us a score card through email of who we, as teachers, should vote for.

Of course, I am not a follower and rarely do what the multitudes dictate. I split my ticket every time, and vote based on who I think can do the best job, as opposed to who gave the union the most lip service. As a teacher, I pay a significant amount of money from my paycheck to union dues. It is in excess of $1,500 annually. Imagine if you will for a moment, how much moolah these unions are raking in. Yet, when I was down and out, they did absolutely nothing for me. It is akin to taxation without representation. I started with my union president. We will call her Karen, for the sake of argument. I had reached out to her the day I had the panic attack and had to leave. I explained the condition I found the classroom in, and how McDickell sent no one to relieve me. She had me email her all of my documentation – doctor's notes, updates, and questions I asked, with no responses from anyone. Days would pass without her answering me either. For a person with heightened anxiety, this was absolute torture. One day, she had me call her on her break. I was pissed – I had no information from anyone. I wasn't getting paid, and my mental health had taken a complete dive. I broke with professionalism and screamed the entire time I was on the phone with her. It smelled suspicious to me. She was shutting me down, or at least attempting to, and I was not having it.

"By the grace of God, no students were hurt in that classroom while I was out!" I roared, "The classroom was beyond vandalized – the kids obviously had weapons of some sort and lighters out in school. How is this even OK?"

My head was throbbing. She – our fearless union president – was acting as if I were the problem. When she told me that the HR director was talking about yanking my teaching certification for "Job Abandonment," I lost it.

"You mean the man who sits on job postings until it's too late to fill them? We have multiple reading teachers placed as long -term substitutes for teachers on maternity leave. How long does it take to post that job? He had months and months of notice! Time and again, he has set me up for failure by not doing his job! Then, I in turn can't do mine. And where does all the sub money go?" I was literally spitting mad.

My throat was raw, and tears pricked my eyes. A vein began to throb mercilessly in my forehead. My rant woke Ella up, and she stumbled into the room, looking scared and confused. But there was no sealing the dam after it broke. I couldn't plug the hole, like the little Dutch boy in the story from my youth.

"And while we are on inept admin making over six figures, let's talk about McDickell! He ruined the last school he was at, so what does our district do? Move him to the best building in the district to fuck that up, too! Where is the accountability? His idea of educational leadership is wandering around the building, discussing beer and sports. We have a superintendent who never leaves her office, and an assistant superintendent who is biding his time until retirement. It's shameful! And dysfunctional! And unethical! In fact, I think the entire district should be placed on an improvement plan by the state!"

At this point, I was breathing harshly, and my voice broke on the last word. I willed myself not to give this imposter the satisfaction of hearing me sob. She audibly gasped at my last statement, feeling the full weight of my words. I won't lie – it felt good to know I struck a nerve. She was retiring at the end of this school year, and her only concern was pushing a contract through.

"A contract with what?" I thought sourly, "The Erebus of Education! That's what" my inner monologue whispered.

"At every turn, our students miss out. They are the true losers and victims here."

That was it. I was spent. My daughter stood looking cautiously at me. Karen seemed to sense the wind down and took the opportunity to tell me she had class to get to and would be in touch.

Every '80s meme was spot on for those my age, but none more so than the satisfaction of slamming a phone down when ending a brutal conversation. Cell phones definitely didn't measure up in that respect. If you slam it when you hang up, it will likely never ring again. I disconnected my cell and sat, staring at it, thinking about what a double-edged sword technology was.

" …. Alright?" I heard Ella say.

"Huh?" I asked, turning my glassy, bloodshot eyes to her.

"Are you alright?" She annunciated each word as if I were a child.

"I taught you to wipe your ass, kid," my inner monologue screamed.

I climb the steps to my bedroom, feeling like I am 90, moving like I am 100. "I'll be fine," I yell back down to Ella as she watches my slow ascent up the steep stairs.

Every bone in my body hurts. My head is throbbing, and my throat aches. As I fall into bed, the bright sunlight hits me in the face and blinds me. My headache swells to migraine status. I pull the blankets over my head and begin to cry.

As the weeks go by, I sink deeper and deeper into depression. I have suffered from postpartum depression with all of my kids. That was bad, but this was worse. Way worse. The hell that deep -seated depression is can only truly be understood by those of us who have lived through it. Sadly, many don't. According to the CDC's website, "Suicide is a leading cause of death in the United States, with 45,979 deaths in 2020. This is about one death every 11 minutes."

(https://www.cdc.gov/suicide/facts/index.html#:~:text=Suicide%20is
%20a%20serious%2
0public,one%20death%20every%2011%20minutes.)

Once again, I will ask, how is this ok? Why do we, as a society, accept this? I would be willing to wager, my Kindreds, that every one of us knows someone who has taken their life whether that be a family member, co-worker, or a friend of a friend. It is just too dang prevalent.

Many times we hear that a person seemed so happy, so well-adjusted, etc. These lost souls are described in eulogies and obituaries as those whose smile "could light up a room." Or perhaps memorializing a special soul that spent umpteen hours volunteering at the SPCA because of an undying love for animals. My Kindreds fully understand what I mean.

For those left behind after a suicide, they will often question why this was such a surprise – why didn't they notice the sadness behind the smile? Survivor's Guilt Syndrome is a real deal, but you know how I say, Kindreds – another topic for another day.

What then of those who are very obviously struggling? Think of all the homeless vets, the neighborhood crazy, or even me. If we, as a society, refuse to acknowledge those in obvious pain, while beating ourselves up over those that we didn't know were in pain, how could we ever hope to save the almost 46,000 souls who gave up the fight in the last year? Because let's face it: that number will most likely jump next year. It doesn't seem to abate. Mental illness is growing at an alarming rate, yet the resources to help it are not.

March came and went, with no resolution to my work situation or my mental health. If anything, I was getting worse. Some days, I couldn't shower or brush my teeth. On other days, I slept because I had been up all night. My sleep patterns were screwed. My meds were increased. Another was added. Then a sleeping pill. My body was in revolt. I threw up everything I ate. If I don't throw up, I shit it out. If this is too graphic, I apologize.

However, this was my daily reality. If I did get out of bed, the room would spin, and I would stumble. I was covered in bruises from this, or walking into walls and furniture. I was seriously like a zombie. I had no doubt my anemia had returned. This only served to make it more difficult to function. I had stopped cooking dinner, shopping, running errands – hell, even cleaning. I rarely left the house. I bit my fingers until they were bloody. When that was too painful, I chewed up the inside of my mouth. I couldn't help it. I didn't even realize when I was doing it. My mouth was covered in ulcers, my skin was sallow, and if only the bags under my eyes held gold.

Weeks went by, and I could not recount even a moment, let alone an hour or a day. I had no idea what the date was. All I could do was wallow. Until the paranoia kicked in, that is. One morning, I sat at the dining room table crying. I could not seem to shake this. I was in the midst of scheduling another gastro appointment, since I couldn't keep anything down. My next step was upping the psych meds again. I was trying to get through one of these calls, and kept hearing a pinging sound in the kitchen. It was really distracting, considering I was trying to stave off hysterics.

As I sat on hold, I kept hearing this pinging sound. It was really bothering me. Finally, I was answered and an appointment was scheduled. The kitchen continued to ping. I disconnected and walked into the kitchen. We have a shelf with a pot rack underneath it to the right. While I watched in wonder, the pots and pans swayed back and forth. The pinging sound I had heard was them banging gently against each other. I stood affixed to the spot. There was no wind - the windows were closed. There were no heating or air conditioning vents in the kitchen: no breeze, no earthquake, nada. For once, the constant rumbling of traffic from behind my house was quiet. Unusually so. I ran into the dining room and grabbed my phone. I fumbled it and cursed myself.

"It won't still be doing that when I get there," I panted, grabbing at the phone.

But I was wrong. A few continued to sway gently back and forth, pinging slowly against each other. I turned on the video and caught a minute or two. This was incredible! Always a fan of ghost shows, I had already debunked anything other than contact. I stood transfixed and watching until they ceased swinging.

"I miss you, Ma," I said softly.

There was no doubt it was my mom. She was always lending me strength at the worst times. I watched the video, and noticed a large orb was flying around the pans. Odd, but that was not visible to the naked eye when I recorded it. It had to be Mom. My heart soared at this thought, and the childlike wonder and amazement I felt made me feel I could handle anything. I knew this feeling would be short-lived, so I picked up the phone again.

Since my union president was doing nothing for me, I decided to climb the PSEA ladder. I insisted on being given the number for the lawyer who handles Southeastern Pennsylvania, where I live and work. She also did nothing basically told me my "hands were tied."

Unsatisfied with this answer, I continued to hound whoever I could. The responses I received were becoming increasingly offensive. My personal favorite was the one union lawyer who told me, "Be creative think outside the box. Isn't that what teachers do?"

Never one to be put off or shut up, I asked her sweetly for an example. She, much like everyone else, blew me off.

Finally, the Long -Term Disability paperwork that I had advocated for arrived. This was a nerve -wracking, tedious process, made more hellish by the fact that my brain was on a permanent vacation. I did my best to take notes whenever I spoke with them or a doctor, but it was useless. I was useless. It had gotten to the point that I needed more help than my family doctor could provide. I was going to a therapist weekly, but these meds were doing more damage than good. My GI issues were insane. Who would want to leave the house when you never knew if you were going to puke or poop? I had no control over it. Much like I had no control over the constant churning in my stomach, sending bile up my throat, and burning my stomach lining. I had filled out the LTD paperwork with Tony's help. The rub was that I had to drop all of it off at the administration center, which housed Human Resources, our superintendent, and the assistant superintendent – all the people I had called out during my last phone call with Karen.

One of the largest issues I had with Karen is that she was a terrible representative for teachers. She usually sided with the admin. Therefore, I suspected that she had informed the upper echelon of our district about what I had said. The fact that the HR head had laid me off was irrefutable evidence in my eyes. That man lived to cover his ass, so if he wasn't pinning this mess on me directly, I knew something was afoot.

In the days leading up to dropping off this paperwork, I was jumping out of my own skin. Who would have thought it was possible to hear electricity? This heightened anxiety always led to upheaval in my GI tract. I had to take Imodium just to make the drive to the admin center. In my distorted mental state, I had become super paranoid.

For the first time in my life, I was glad masks were still mandated in our buildings. I decided to add sunglasses, a ski hat with my hair tucked up underneath, and bulky clothing. This assured my hapless self that no one would recognize me. I waited for my voice of reason to object, but there was silence.

"Mom," I called out, "If ever I needed you, it's now."

I wanted to cry, but I knew that was a slippery slope that would lead to me never dropping off this paperwork. I swallowed down the tears and headed for the car.

My plan was to drop off the envelope to the secretary and roll. As I started the car, I was practicing my deep breathing to stave off a panic attack. I couldn't take the emergency meds and drive, so it was time to yank on those bootstraps.

When the radio came on, Fleetwood Mac's *The Chain* was playing. The timing, band, and choice of song were not lost on me. It was my mom letting me know she was there to support me. There wasn't much traffic this time of day. I changed the station, and Fleetwood Mac came on again. Maybe it sounds as crazy as I was at the time, but I could feel Mom's presence. It settled me a little as much as I could be in my current state of panic. I arrived much sooner than I expected. I turned off the car and did some more breathing. When I exited the car and reached the door, it was locked. I almost cried as I rang the doorbell in vain. Finally, a nice young black woman came to the door. She explained that the entry system wasn't working properly.

"Nothing in this district does," said my inner voice. I couldn't disagree.

Typically, a dour -faced old white woman was the secretary, and I expected to hand it off to her. This lady wouldn't take the envelope and called the HR secretary. My stomach lurched.

"Do not puke. Do not puke," was all I could say to myself. Imagine that inside a mask! The HR lady arrived just as someone was trying to buzz in through the broken door. It created the perfect amount of distraction. I was able to hand the envelope off to HR and skulk out the door. By the time I got to the car, I was pulling in deep, yet ragged breaths. I started the car, and guess what came on? If you chose Fleetwood Mac, you would be correct, Kindreds. I made my way home, feeling a tiny bit lighter. At last, I heard back from the LTD lady. I was approved, she said. A deposit would be made to my bank account; however, it was recommended that I see a psychiatrist.

"This is a mental health disability," she informed me.

The old me would have felt shame at that statement; however, the new me could have cared less. All I knew was that I could pay some of the bills I was way behind on.

After searching the hovel that had become my house, I found my work-issued laptop. I fired it up and logged onto my insurance website. I knew I wanted a woman doctor, so I found one semi-close to my house (in case it was a day when I couldn't drive) that was accepting new patients. I called and made an appointment.

They emailed me the intake paperwork I was to fill out before my first appointment. I looked it over in dismay; the attachment they sent was in excess of twenty pages. My vision was flooded with tears. How the hell was I expected to fill any of this out with an iota of accuracy when I couldn't even brush my hair? I slammed the computer closed and dissolved into a puddle of tears.

"We are not meant to win this game," my inner voice chided.

"Fuck you," I growled out loud.

I hated myself just as much as I despised this new obstacle – one in a seemingly unending line of obstacles. I just wanted to lie down and not wake up.

"Take all the pills," a voice said. This was a new voice in my head.

It wasn't my internal monologue, that voice that was always there, just below the surface. You may know what I mean, you may not. My internal monologue allowed me to make decisions by weighing the pros and cons. It gave me gut instincts, second thoughts, pauses, and questions that I might have breezed through otherwise without much thought. The brain is such an amazing organ – it does all of this without us even recognizing it. My inner voice warned me when someone or something felt off. Many of us have this voice; it can be called an inner monologue, a conscience, a guardian angel, a gut instinct, or whatever. This was not that.

I tilted my head to the side to hear better. I pictured my dog Scooby doing this, and felt foolish. The voice was silent.

"Did I really hear that?" I wondered.

Followed on the heels of this thought came another: "Why would I hear that?"

Did I really want to end it, I wondered?

"Not now," my inner voice sighed.

A vague, gauzy thought occurred to my feeble mind: was my usual voice acquainted with this other, new, alien voice that sounded so negative? And if so, why didn't I know? After all, I was the keeper of the voices, the vessel.

"I should have known," I yelled out, my hands balled into fists. I looked around the room wildly. There was no answer.

"I am really losing it," I muttered to myself. I trudged towards the shower, whacking my hip against the dresser.

"That'll leave a mark," someone said, I am unsure who.

All I wanted was a long, hot shower, because that relieved some of my muscle aches. My muscles ache constantly from being so uptight 24/7. In fact, my jaw aches because my teeth are clenched all night when I sleep, or attempt to. I stumbled into the bathroom and promptly slammed my finger while shutting the bathroom door. I slowly climbed into the shower, because it was my safe space to cry in.

It's hard to pinpoint my Kindreds or fully describe the range of emotions I was feeling. I was confused, angry, sad, hurt, despondent, disappointed, yet detached, physically ill, and exhausted to my core. I sat in the shower with my knees pulled up to my chest, the scalding hot water beating down on me. I ugly cried, as if I had been beaten with the ugly stick a thousand times over.

"It might feel better to be beaten," My now weak monologue voice croaked. Or was that the other voice? I couldn't tell anymore, and this made me cry harder.

"You sound like a dying Orca," the voice I used to know, and had taken for granted, chanted along with this new voice.

Chapter 7

Summer arrived in full force. In the world at large, Ukraine was still under attack by Russia, Trump was still being investigated regarding the insurrection, and Biden was our president. Not typically a politically motivated person, I marveled at the mess our world had become.

As a teacher in a low-income school district, it was still not lost on me that our youth rallies against the patriarchy, yet that was exactly what our presidency was. We had two old white dudes as our choices.

"None of them are fit to serve," I thought to myself.

What a farce the US had become. I barely recognized my own country anymore, and that simply served to push me further down the well of despair. My father was a Marine and spent his entire life as a government mule. The first song I learned was *"The Battle Hymn of the Republic" at the age of two or three*. We were patriots to the core. My dad had one tattoo, and that was the bust of a soldier bearing the cross of Jesus. Underneath, it read "For God, country, and family." Those were the principles I was raised with. Those are the principles that seem to be popular to neglect, or outright reject, no matter what higher power you believe in. Civil service was a way of life in my family. My uncle is a Corps lifer. He retired as a Gunnery Sergeant. My other uncle was a lifer in the Army National Guard. My father -in-law was a career Navy man. His grandson followed in his footsteps. Tony also has two brothers who were in the Corps. One died a Marine at 38 years of age, and was buried with full military honors like my dad. Another grandson did two tours with the Corps. Our patriotic roots run deep on both sides of our family.

Therefore, I felt despair over what was happening in the good 'ol US of A. The media was toxic and biased, spoon-feeding us what they believe we need to hear. My mother would have despised what journalism has become. This little nugget of wisdom did nothing to lift my mood. I may be treading water, dipping under occasionally, but so far, I haven't drowned.

"Maybe today is the day you finally do," said the negative one.

I flipped off my reflection in the mirror and turned off the TV. I went downstairs and stood before the sink full of overflowing dishes in the kitchen. I gazed out the window. Today, I felt there might be a light at the end of the tunnel. That is yet another cruel twist of depression: you can have a day—or even a week—when you feel more like your old self than you have in a while. You sense a sliver of hope, like maybe you actually will pull out of this.

When in reality, it is like the rug being pulled out from under you when you have just gained your footing. Bam! Just as you least expect it, depression rears its hideous head, and you are back under. Maybe only for a night, or maybe for a month.

"Maybe forever," sighed the new voice.

She surely was seductive. When she wasn't being snarky, which wasn't often, her voice sounded like silk rustling or leaves blowing in the wind. Usually, I just get pissed off at it/her. Yet, the allure was unique. That voice was coated in the velvet of underground darkness, like a poisonous moss that willed me to lie down with it.

"I could see all the stars," I thought dreamily.

Now, I was gazing at the knife block to my right for what felt like a long time. I caressed it with my gaze and thought about the satisfying sound the knives made when they slid out of the self-sharpening block. I remembered how the blade would gleam in the overhead lights as I chopped up ingredients for dinner.

"And when was the last time you cooked dinner?" this new voice mocked.

Boy, she certainly could change in a second.

My constant failure to be a proper wife was on my growing list of concerns. I knew it, yet I wasn't doing much to change it. How could I when I could barely groom myself? It's impossible to pick each other up when everyone is down and out. Summer was my only solace, besides my beautiful grandson. I had done quite a bit of babysitting since leaving work, and I credited him as the reason I was still hanging on. Plus, summer was my favorite season. It wasn't just because I was a teacher. I was born on Memorial Day, and in our parts, this signified the unofficial start to summer.

Many, many Philly and Delco peeps would head "down the shore," and our area would settle down. I hadn't been going out much, as I said earlier. Everywhere was just "too peopley" for me. That's why I loved the mountains – it was so less congested than Philly or Delco. We had been lucky enough to hold onto both places throughout this ordeal, and I needed some time in the mountains.

There was still a pall over the cabin when I went there. I had been up since my Mom died- hell, I was responsible for cleaning out, listing, and selling her mountain place. That was its own personal hell in itself. I cried, puked, and danced with full-blown panic attacks every time I went there.

Her whole life was packed in to this tiny mountain home, and I had the pleasure of sorting through it all and deciding where it would go. Thank heavens for my brothers, my sister -in-law, my kids, and, most of all, Tony. I marveled time and again how the hell he put up with me. He was my anchor, and I am so very thankful for him.

Luckily, my step father went and stayed in New York with his son. This made cleaning out slightly easier – silver linings and all that. He was simply waiting for the house to sell, so he could make his next move.

Every time I went to my mother's, I cried hard. It was a trigger for me, this house I had found for her, which was absolutely perfect in so many ways. It was all on one floor, because she couldn't do steps. It had a large kitchen, and she loved to cook. The bathroom had a shower stall and a whirlpool tub. My mom loved to lounge in a tub, reading. She had made it her own. In fact, she had just made the last payment on her new bedroom set right before she passed. She was so proud of all the new furnishings, rugs, and curtains. She had purchased all brand-new appliances for the kitchen. And a deep freezer for her cookies.

The house still smelled like her, and that was a curse as well as a blessing. I missed her so much that my heart felt as if it had been ripped from my chest. I was no longer whole, in more ways than one. I am an orphan now. My parents are gone. I thought back to years ago when my Nan passed. She was my mother's mother. My mom cried about being an orphan then, and I recall thinking, "Geez, Ma, you are in your '60s. It's bound to happen."

Little did I know then, age didn't matter. I felt exactly as I imagined she had felt that day so many long years ago. These thoughts, of course, brought tears. They were never far behind my eyes anyhow. When I looked in the mirror, all I saw were big, bloodshot, glassy eyes that no longer looked like my own. Thankfully, I didn't have the haunted look Aaron got when he was in crisis. I have cried every day since Mom died. Sometimes more than once a day. It seemed as if the ache would never cease. I hoped the appointment with the new psychiatrist would help. I was not typically a crier. That role was reserved for funerals and the like. I wanted to go back to being that bad ass.

It was scary, though I actually envied my mom. She was with so many of our lost loved ones, and this? This wasn't living, it was existing. I didn't need the new, negative voice to tell me that. It felt like there was somewhere I needed or wanted to be, but it wasn't here. As the prolific, underground genius Charles Bukowski penned, "I want so much that is not here. And I do not know where to go." This feeling could only be described by the Scottish term "Hiraeth." If you don't know it, make sure you look it up.

Since the pandemic, many doctors have continued to work virtually. My new psychiatrist was one. I cued up my laptop and sat on the edge of my bed. She connected to the virtual room, and I observed that she was a thin, middle-aged, Middle Eastern woman. She listened to my story, interrupting occasionally to ask questions. She nodded sympathetically at all the right parts. She prescribed an increase in my current medication, Zoloft. She also suggested going to an intensive outpatient program through her employer, Malmore. I declined and took the med increase. She would see me online in a month.

"Malmore," I thought. "That's that drug place. It's a rehab."

This was my regular inner monologue, and I was helluva glad for it.

"Not ever happening," I said aloud, in my own, authentic voice that had been quiet for so long now. I was disappointed that that was all that was being offered.

"There is no cure for mental illness," the negative voice spat out. "It's permanent," she added for spite.

Lately, I have been reflecting on what it means to hear more than one voice. My son, Aaron, heard voices when he was in crisis, and also when he was leading up to or coming down from a crisis. That was schizophrenia, though. I had begun researching it when he was first diagnosed. I not only wanted to understand what he was going through, but I also wanted answers on how I could best help him.

"There are no answers," the negative one stated.

I knew it wasn't what Aaron had. That manifested young, and I wasn't.

"Your mind broke. It took years, but it finally snapped. And now you will never be you again!" Both voices this time. I headed to CVS to get this new prescription.

"Sure, you can drive today?" mocked just the new voice. "Lots of twists and turns up here," she sneered.

"Enough!" I screamed. I put my hands to the side of my head. What the hell had happened to me? I was a well-respected educator with tenure and a master's.

"Well, you used to be well-respected," she scoffed, despite my warning. I turned up the music to drown out any more.

The next morning, I woke up with a song in my head. This was not unusual for me. I have marveled many times before how fortunate I was to wake to internal music. It wasn't typically the same song, and it wasn't every single day. But it was enough days to warrant joy. Today's selection, probably a la negative one, was "Hello Darkness My Old Friend." If you are truly a Kindred, you know the tune.

"I always come to talk to you again," I muttered, meandering towards the bathroom. The body aches persisted. My back hurts all the time, no matter how often I visit the chiropractor. Lately, my old hairdresser's knees were adding to the agony. Some days it was the Trifecta of Pure Pain: back, knees, and neck. On other days, the players changed their legs, shoulders, and feet. It reminded me of the song I would sing with my grandson "Head, Shoulders, Knees and Toes."

I cackled out loud. It occurred to me, and not for the first time, that I sounded crazy.

"Crazy is as crazy does," the voices sang.

It was early July, and our annual family vacation was coming up. I was feeling excited for something for the first time in an eon, it seemed. Then the call came. Tony's older brother had been battling stomach cancer for over a year. It had come time to say our goodbyes.

With Covid still lurking about, the whole unit of us five couldn't go at once. We decided the oldest, Angelica, would go with Tony and me to see him. Aaron and Ella would follow Sunday when they both had off. They would stop there and then meet us at the cabin for vacation. He lived about 45 minutes away from us. We made the drive in silence.

Always my mother's daughter, I came loaded down with food for them. When we arrived, he was in a hospital bed in the family room. He wasn't really conscious, but he could hear us and weakly squeezed Tony's hand. Much as I had done with my mom, I stood to the side, slowly stroking what was left of his hair. None of us wanted to overstay our welcome, and we gave Tony privacy at the end of our visit.

All three of us cried on the way home. So much loss in such a short time, I thought sadly. My heart broke yet again, but this time for my family. For my husband and my kids. For my mother and father-in-law, and above all, for his wife and children.

Everyone. I just hurt for everyone. On top of the daily hurt. On top of the anxiety. On top of the depression.

"It's a volatile cocktail," mused my inner voice.

"Or a suicide cocktail," offered the negative one.

Since the family vacation started Saturday, Tony and I went up to the cabin on Friday. We ran errands, getting food, ice, and alcohol, everything we needed to be comfortable and have fun. We were looking forward to spending time around the campfire and in the pool with our grandson. The next day, we got up early and did the lawn, raked the leaves, and swept up fallen wood to burn. In the forest, there were always branches down. Most we left, to return to the soil. We had just cracked open our reward for all the hard work when the phone rang —my phone. I looked down at it. My sister-in-law was calling. I looked to my husband. He didn't have his phone.

"Oh no," I said. I answered the phone. She was crying.

"I won't make you say the words," I told her.

We sobbed for a few minutes, then hung up the phone. I turned to Tony, "I am so sorry, babe." I was openly crying. I didn't have to say anymore. He knew.

For the second time in less than six months, we made calls to our kids to let them know a family member had passed. Angelica postponed coming until the next day. Aaron and Ella were heartbroken that they didn't get to say "goodbye" again. Tony and I drank ourselves into a stupor, crying occasionally, each lost in our own thoughts. We then went to bed.

At midweek, we packed up and came home for the funeral. It was terribly sad, as expected. I tried to say all the right things, but my head felt full of cotton.

"You're a cotton-headed ninny muggins," said my old internal voice, and just her. I stifled a giggle. The movie *Elf* was a favorite of both my mother and me.

My sister-in-law was the epitome of gentility, and I don't know how she pulled it off. Her sons and daughter followed suit. They had been married almost as long as Tony and I had been. That bond doesn't break. It bleeds.

Our entire family got through the day with dignity. The readings, flowers, and pictures all bespoke a life well lived. Yet, it was becoming obvious at both of these funerals that we had to suffer through, that our families were dwindling in size. It wasn't the first time I mourned this, but it felt more urgent this time. We needed some grace so badly —all of us. My grandson provided a bit of much-needed comedic relief at the luncheon, running around and giggling like the dickens. He was so loved, and I prayed the world wouldn't ruin his innocent charm, his inquisitive nature.

We drove back to the cabin that night, all of us, in a caravan of vehicles.

"I'll do it for the caravan," I thought to myself in my best broken Irish, mimicking Brad Pitt. (If you know, you know my Kindreds.)

This ability to draw parallels between movies I have seen and real life is a little gift I like to call "Cinematic Tourette's." As the meme says, "If you can't handle my random references to movies I've seen, we can't be friends." I use Tourette's not to belittle those that suffer from it, but to illustrate how ingrained it was in me just to do this. I had been doing it since I was a kid. It's this same habit that had me quoting *ELF* to myself at the funeral. No doubt, it is a coping mechanism, even if ill-suited. I, unlike others, own my shiz.

Most people have their ways of dealing with loss, grief, heartache, and trauma. My go-to was dark humor and sarcasm. It felt good to be able to fall back on an old habit that, even if grossly inappropriate at times, was a piece of the old me that I was grasping onto. We all have our life buoys, and this was one of mine. I wasn't hurting anyone; is the way I looked at it. Plus, I had the decency to know when to keep it to myself.

We made the best of the rest of the vacation, but our hearts just weren't in it. My therapist said to keep looking for the "silver linings," so I decided to be grateful we were all together to mourn. It seemed that was all we did anymore.

At the end of July, I had my next telehealth appointment with the Malmore doctor.

She had double-booked somehow and told me she couldn't see me until August. Uncomfortable with this potential arrangement, I asked her to just check in with a phone call when she had a few free moments. She did, and I was told to keep taking the meds, that I hadn't even seen the full effects of the increased dose yet. Lord knows I desperately needed it, because this was at the pinnacle of cleaning my mom's house out.

That August, I received a call from the LTD lady. She apparently had sent paperwork to be filled out by this psychiatrist, and she hadn't received any of it back.

"We need updates on your progress in order to keep providing benefits," she stated.

In layman's terms, if the psychiatrist didn't return these papers, I wasn't getting paid anymore. I already had my income reduced by 40%.

Add to that, I was still carrying the health insurance and paying out of pocket for it, and we were hurt piece. I couldn't lose this disability payment, or we would likely end up homeless. Tony could only carry so much. Yes, he was doing a bang-up job at it, but the chinks in his armor were starting to show. When the day arrived for my psych appointment, I was apprehensive about the LTD paperwork.

"Why wouldn't she tell me last month that she had these papers and no intention of filling them out?" I asked myself. I waited for a snarky reply from the negative one. Nothing came.

My GI issues had been on Defcon 10 since the start of cleaning out my mom's. My brain remained full of cotton, and I was struggling to focus. I found myself sitting or standing in the house, staring at nothing. I was never sure how long I had been like that, since time had ceased to exist for me. Doctor appointments were the only thing that reminded me of the constraints of time.

Unfortunately for me, I always tended to forgetfulness, but now I was akin to an Alzheimer's patient. I didn't know if I was coming or going; I couldn't remember anything, and I was constantly searching for things I had misplaced. I had watched my Nan die from this vicious disease of the brain, and it was not lost on me how much I was like her at the end of her life in those dark days.

When the doctor connected to our telehealth, she asked how I was. I was honest that I was struggling. She asked what was so hard for me, and I started to explain about cleaning out my mom's. She abruptly cut me off and asked me a question. I wasn't done answering her first question when she shot out another. I was beginning to feel very overwhelmed.

This led me to inquire about the LTD paperwork, and she informed me she "did not feel comfortable filling that out."

I asked why, and she responded that "she didn't know me well enough."

I argued with her to the best of my ability, "This isn't our first appointment, you have been my doctor all summer!" I yelled, losing my cool.

She ignored me and suggested I have my GI doctor fill it out. "You are experiencing an uptick in those symptoms," was her reasoning.

"I am under a mental health disability, he can't fill it out," I tried to explain, but was now crying.

"I am going to prescribe intensive outpatient services through Malmore," she said, scribbling furiously on her legal pad, "and the maximum allowable dosage of the Zoloft."

I was scared and unsure. My vision started to swim, and I was having a hard time breathing.

"No! I will not do that," I responded.

"Well, your therapy doesn't seem to be helping, hmmm?" She replied flippantly.

At this point, I was visibly upset and openly sobbing. I tried again to explain myself, but she cut me off and told me she was calling my family doctor, as I was being "noncompliant."

She then proceeded to end the session. I was shocked. What the hell had just happened? I lay down on my bed to cry. My therapist appointment – also Telemed – was scheduled for that afternoon. I had calmed myself down somewhat by then and related to her all that had transpired. She was also shocked and super sympathetic.

"I am so sorry that happened to you," she said softly.

Tina really was a calming influence in my life. She helped me to see things I couldn't, and she pushed me towards more holistic approaches than just meds. That was why I liked and trusted her so much. Plus, it was healing to be validated.

"That was extremely unprofessional," she continued. "Can I help with this paperwork?" she asked.

I wasn't sure that the LTD people would accept that since she technically wasn't a doctor. However, she knew me better than the bitch that had just hung up on me, and honestly, what choice did I have?

"Thank you so very much, Tina," I said.

We planned to meet next week in her office to complete it. She ended the session by helping me with my breathing exercises.

As is my life, when one ray of sunshine pokes its head through, the clouds are never far behind. I had no sooner disconnected from therapy when my cell phone rang. It was my family doctor's office, calling to make an appointment with me. I reluctantly agreed to be there the next morning.

Of course, I was so amped up that night, sleep eluded me yet again. It is difficult to explain the horrors your overactive imagination can perpetrate on you when you top it off with severe depression and anxiety, plus panic attacks —the cherry on my psycho sundae.

Those long, dark hours were only broken by the visits to the bathroom. Many nights, I slept with a trash can next to me, in case the immediate need to vomit came. It often did, and tonight was no exception. Honestly, I didn't know what to expect at the doctor's, but the way it did go down – I could not have imagined it in my worst nightmares.

First, I expected to have Lena, not Dr. Lowes. I always had Lena. In fact, the first time in eight years I had met my family doctor was when my mom died. He had been warm and kind then. He was anything but on this day. When he walked into the room, he shut the door and told me to remove my mask. He sat down and asked me point-blank what I was doing.

At least he let me explain my side without interrupting me with a barrage of questions, like my supposed psychiatrist had done. His reaction was not what I had hoped for. He had been so supportive last time I had seen him that I guess I just expected a similar experience. This was not that.

He asked why I thought I knew better than a doctor.

"I definitely know myself better than she does. She said it herself she doesn't know me well enough to fill out my LTD paperwork, but in the same breath tells me she knows me well enough to know I need intensive outpatient therapy? Sorry, doc, I ain't buying what she is selling. This is an obvious ploy to get another referral for Malmore. She probably gets a kick back."

He didn't like this answer and decided to play devil's advocate.

"But again, you are telling me you know better than a woman with a doctorate." He sounded exasperated. I took umbrage at this statement.

"I have three college diplomas, doc. I am hardly stupid. I just know myself. I will be so anxious about this that I will be up all night, in the bathroom with GI problems. I would probably fall asleep in therapy. Not to mention, it's mostly druggies there.

Malmore is known for that. Not that I have anything against druggies," I went on, now rambling.

"But they aren't on my wavelength. Their therapy isn't mine."

He was looking at my records on the computer, and I appeared to have lost his interest.

"Plus, my husband and daughter work across the street. I see the patients walk in every day." I was still driving Ella to work daily because her accident remained unsettled.

"They look like mostly rebellious teens. Can you see me in a group with a bunch of kids complaining about how awful their parents are? I have real-life problems, doc. This is not for me, and I am smart enough to know that. I know my limitations. I researched my mental illness – I am a teacher that's what we do. There are many approaches to what I have, and she is mandating one. I want a doctor who is a partner on this mental health journey with me, not some overlord decreeing what I have to do! Did you also know she wants to up my meds to the maximum allowable dosage under FDA law?"

My voice broke on the last word. I was getting worked up, and that would only prove that witch's point. I struggled to get myself under control. This seemed to catch his attention. He had been nonchalantly perusing my history on his computer while I talked. He looked at me over his glasses and admitted he didn't think that was a good idea.

"But I agree with everything else she said," he continued, "this isn't going to go well with you and Long-Term Disability if you are refusing treatment."

Well, now, there was a side I didn't see. "Crap," said my internal voice.

"You think you are so smart with your multiple diplomas," mimicked the negative one.

"Well, my therapist agrees with me, and she is filling the papers out for me," I spat back at him, as much as at the overtly negative voice that was now living rent-free in my head.

"Good," he answered, standing up and signaling he was done with me. "I am going to have to talk to Lena about filling out paperwork for patients," he warned me.

"Great, now you got that nice nurse practitioner in trouble with her boss," mocked the negative one.

I looked at him as I gathered my belongings. Tears began to slide down my cheeks.

"Well, I guess we have to agree to disagree, doc, but mental health in this country is a Goddamn mess. It's a disgrace this is where I am and …. and … I can't get the help I seek," I sputtered.

I walked out of his office, full on crying. I pulled my mask up and headed for the stairs, avoiding the elevator. I didn't want anyone to see me crying, and God forbid someone ask me if I was okay. Isn't it odd how, when you really need someone to be nice to you, it's preferable to avoid it because you are afraid of how you will dissolve into a puddle of tears at the first sign of sympathy?

"Mental health is an absolute bitch to deal with, but let's jump through multiple hoops while trying to survive!" My inner voice raged while I made my way to the parking lot.

"Let's be real. You couldn't handle any of this on your best day," intoned the negative one.

As I got into the car, she offered a final parting shot: "You are the opposite of King Midas. Everything you touch turns to shit instead of gold."

Chapter 8

When I met with Tina, she went over our allotted time, helping me with the LTD papers. She promised to fax them right over for me. I left her office feeling grateful and slightly less defeated.

Upon arriving home, I dug out my laptop and started a new search for a psychiatrist. I found a woman and called to schedule an appointment with her. I gave her the run down – switching doctors, already on medication, needed guidance on the medication.

More paperwork was sent, and I went about the slow task of trying to understand it. My focus had not improved, and my cognitive skills were lacking. This was supremely frustrating for one who had always relied on her wits. It took me most of the day, because I found myself reading the same sentences over and over without retaining any information. I managed to finish it and return it. My first appointment is next week. I had to remain hopeful. It wasn't easy, and I lost the battle with that goal daily, but Aaron and I made a pact to lift each other up. He was still struggling, and I was currently the only one who understood at all. We spent a lot of days together back then, and he was good company for a mentally distressed mom.

Although I rarely ventured out of the house, it was a necessary evil. I wished I could order everything online, but it wasn't feasible with as many people as I was feeding. Additionally, there were trips to the post office, gas station, and bank when they could no longer be avoided. It was on one of these mundane trips that I committed a giant blunder. A major gaffe.

In my defense, I was still a hot mess. I was running errands and tended to visit shopping centers where I could get everything in almost one stop. Gone were the days of Trader Joe's and BJ's. My family was lucky that I was making an effort at all, that's how I viewed it.

So, here I am at Kohl's again. I love Kohl's. So did my mom. Where else can you spend money and walk out with more free money? Kohl's cash is the jawn. Only certain Kindreds will understand that reference, because after all, "It's a Philly thing."

Again, considering that I couldn't walk and chew gum, it was a miracle I could even run an errand. Few as they were, most were successful. This one was not.

When I finished shopping and got to my car, my keys were gone. I searched the ground around my vehicle. Nothing. I tore my purse apart. Nothing. I checked every pocket. Nada. Due to my mental state, I immediately started having trouble breathing. All of a sudden, it was way too bright outside.

Since I suddenly couldn't see, I retreated back to the store. I went to the Lost and Found. No keys. I retraced my footsteps, no keys. I was on the ground, looking under displays. All to no avail. Now I was truly panicking. I went outside again to see if I could find them. Maybe they rolled under another car? I had no idea. As I got on my hands and knees in the parking lot, I was pulling in deep, noisy breaths.

"Seriously?" the negative one said. "You can't run a simple errand without it turning into *Days of Our Lives*."

This was an old soap opera my Nan had watched when I was a kid. Once more, the old ways came through. Whereas before they had been a source of comfort, this hated voice was twisting it all up.

My goddaughter answered that she was off and not far away. She said she would be there soon. I sat on the bench outside the store, waiting. I flitted between crying silently and looking despondently towards my vehicle.

Luckily, not many people were shopping during the work hours. Unfortunately, the nurse from my doctor's office was one. I had recently had a negative encounter there, and didn't need her to see me crying on a bench, so I scurried away and headed back to the parking lot.

"What are the chances?" I asked myself.

"But of course, you attract what you are," piped up Ms. Negativity, "and that is fucked up!"

She began to cackle, and it echoed in my ears as well as my head. Her mirthless laugh reverberated in my old, silver fillings. My limbs shook, and I was dizzy. I stumbled, temporarily blinded, as my skin crawled, my stomach churned, and my mind screamed "Leave me alone!"

As I stumbled, head down, still scanning for my keys, a car pulled up next to me.

It was the same color, model, and make as my goddaughter's (Kellie). Without thinking, I walked over and opened the back door. Or at least I attempted to. They were locked at first. The windows were tinted, so it was hard to see who was in there or what was going on. The driver, in her confusion, meant to check that the doors were locked when I reached for them.

However, she panicked and hit the door lock twice, granting me access. Oblivious to the fact that this was not Kellie's car, I opened up the back door. T wo teenage girls were sitting in the backseat. They were approximately the same age as Kellie's sister, Sara, so I assumed they were her friends. She was in the front passenger seat while Kellie drove.

That was a very incorrect assumption, Kindreds. This was not a car that belonged to anyone in my family, even though it was identical to the one that was picking me up.

Undeterred, I tried to get in the backseat after opening the door.

"Squeeze a cheek?" I asked the horrified young girls. I meant "move over," but the damage was done before I even knew what was up.

"Noooooo!" screamed the mom, turning in her driver's seat to face me at the back door of their car.

"Get out! Get out! Get out!" she kept screaming, very obviously thinking I was a sex trafficker or something crazy like that.

I backed away from the car, not quite comprehending what was happening. I kept muttering "I'm sorry" as I retreated.

One more time, I turned and went back into Kohl's. This time, I went directly to the first register and meekly inquired about lost keys. The cashier smiled at me and produced my keys. I almost fell to my knees with gratitude. As she handed them to me, I saw the mom and girls come in. She looked warily at me, and I turned to her, smiling.

"See, I just lost my keys. My ride has the same car as yours."

She looked at me as if I were a pariah, and hurried her kids along far away from me. Briefly, I wondered why she still looked at me as if I were a dirty leper, even when I proved I wasn't Chester the Molester.

"Because you're broken and everyone can see it," observed the negative one.

I waited for my inner voice to stick up for me. She didn't. I drove home without finishing my errands. Kellie was pulling in as I was pulling out. I didn't tell her what had happened. I made my way home slowly, sobbing the entire way.

"Next time, perhaps they will lock you up," she continued as I pulled into the driveway. "You should be anyhow."

Not disagreeing with this bleak bitch was hard. Cynicism was oxygen for me, as was sarcasm. This was most certainly not that. Instead, this was prodding and probing.

Almost like a rotten tooth. You know it's there, and sure you will make a dentist appointment pronto. Meanwhile, you hold off because dentists are for those who have time and money. Inevitably, your tongue finds its way to that source of rot, that decay. This voice, the negative one, is the source of misery, anguish, and horror, but also truth. She was the serpent's tongue, the mouthpiece. Her opinions grew stronger, while my inner companion grew dimmer.

"I am the vessel," I told myself. "I dictate what my outcome is."

Her references always started as veiled and progressively got more aggressive. Even in my weakened mental state, I knew this to be true. My stubbornness was, for once, an asset.

Conversely, the appointment with my new psychiatrist renewed all hope. She was a kind, soft-spoken black woman, probably about my age. Her name was Dr. Merry. I filled her in on everything. She displayed shock when I told her why I left my other psychiatrist. She asked a lot of questions about my GI disorder and seemed thorough.

"I am surprised that your other doctor kept increasing your Zoloft, since it is notorious for causing these types of GI issues," she informed me.

"But of course she did," replied my inner voice.

We wrapped up with an overhaul of meds and an appointment for two weeks. I thanked her and disconnected from Telemed. I digested what she had just told me. I could have been off this medication and on something else that wouldn't exacerbate the GI problems.

"That uppity witch!" my inner voice seethed, "Not only did she not help you, but she very likely would have made you worse."

No chorus from the negative one today. I sincerely hoped that was the beginning of a trend. Summer was waning. As always, I was sorry to see it go. My family had always marked the end of glorious, sunny summer with a crab fest. My mom's shore place was where it was held annually, but we had done it up in the mountains last year.

"If only I had known it was our last one," I mourned.

The ache of missing my mom never left me, not even for a moment. We had so many unfulfilled plans. We had been blessed with a perfect baby, and she wasn't here to enjoy him. It tore at my soul. I often talked to my mom out loud, wishing she would visit me in a dream. Things had been quiet on that front for quite some time. Until she dropped another major sign on me, that is. I finished cleaning out her place and needed to get away from the mountain for a while. I needed to decompress and be inside four different walls, so I went back to Delco.

Over a month had passed since I had last been at her grave site. I decided to grab some roses and go see her. My emergency meds had been used more times than I could count that summer. That day was no exception. Luckily, Dr. Merry provided me with some that didn't make me as woozy and toasty.

It was odd because the radio in my vehicle hadn't worked in years. This didn't bother me because I had a subscription to satellite radio. I never turned on the FM radio; it was either set to Sirius or off. On that particular day, it was off. Loud noises had really started to get to me. Music was sometimes in that category, depending on my mental state – which wasn't great that day.

Anyhow, I pull up to the section she is buried in, and I left my Jeep running. I got out and just stood at her grave, ugly crying. It was the sort of grief that froze your lungs even as the sobs were escaping. The sobbing was the deep, guttural type, that kind that comes from the soul.

Again, I could feel my heart actually rending in my chest, and I couldn't breathe. I was yelling too, but I don't remember what. Thankfully, I was alone in the cemetery, or the police probably would have been called. I know full well I looked and sounded crazy, but I didn't care.

Finally, I stumbled to the car. My vision was swimming, and dots were circling. I climbed in and rooted around the glove compartment for napkins to clean the snot off myself. It was then that I realized the radio was blaring. I couldn't quite comprehend what was happening.

"What the hell?" asked my inner voice.

As I listened, it became apparent this was a gospel station. A choir was singing about being with the Father, being home, and being at peace. The song ended, and the station's call handle came on. It was called "ALIVE FM."

Suddenly, I felt calm. The sobs stopped, my heart rate slowed, and my vision came back into focus I wiped down my face, and put the jeep in gear. As I slowly drove home, I kept that station on I have no recollection of what songs were played. I just knew that I felt less alone that I had in a long time.

Chapter 9

One of my beliefs was that you could be a spiritual person without being religious. Many people confuse these two and tend to think of them as synonymous. They aren't.

For me, spirituality was a means towards inner peace, and religion was not. For people who preached forgiveness and loving thy neighbor, organized religion practiced anything but. The hypocrisy was abounding and obvious when you looked for it. Gays, LGBTQ, and anyone else who didn't fit their mold were not only discarded but demonized. That was not love. Therefore, it wasn't for me.

Think for a moment, how many wars have been waged in the name of religion. How many people have died because of organized religions? I am not only speaking on the Crusades, extremists, and such, but what about those poor, lost souls I discussed earlier? Religion and the lack of acceptance to be found there when one does not fit the model are most certainly responsible for a dearth of suicides. Especially when you consider the pedophile priests. For as many as we know publicly of, there are many more we don't. Or let's talk about honor killings and stoning. Archaic as it sounds, it is still happening in the world. All in the name of religion.

When you make the move from religious adherence to spirituality, it all shifts.

Once the veil of religiosity has been lifted, one looks at life differently. It is a shedding of the narrow views of the church and an acceptance of life in all its forms. When this rebirth happens, an inner peace is achieved. Does this mean I am healed? If only. What it did mean was I was approaching life and its many obstacles differently. This in itself was healing to an extent. There is so much more that goes along with this mindset, but again, another topic for another day.

Even so, it was draining trying to get through all these "firsts" without my mom. Mother's Day was banned in my house, as I chose not to celebrate it.

"Maybe next year," I told my family with a sad smile.

I didn't celebrate my birthday either. It was the first time in my entire life that I didn't get a cake from my mom. The only thing I missed more than her cooking was her company.

Labor Day gave way to fall, and I thought again about how much I missed the classroom. I missed having a purpose, besides just surviving. I continued my therapy and my med schedule. The GI issues were improving. Dr. Merry was exactly what I had been searching for: she was knowledgeable, sympathetic, and actually listened to me.

Instead of ordering me to do things, she asked my opinion on the treatment options she offered. She was the partner I had been searching for to help me overcome this paralyzing anxiety and get me back to being me.

"Or whatever I am when this is all over," observed my inner monologue. At least, I hoped it stayed a monologue.

There always seems to be another shoe to drop, though. This time it was

Angelica. Her partner had assaulted her and thrown a cinder block through her car window. She pressed charges, but was informed it was only a misdemeanor and he would be out on the street in a few hours. If they found him, that was. It never ceases to amaze me how messed up our system is here in America. I went over and cleaned up her car the best I could. We packed up clothes and whatever else the baby would need and headed back to my house.

Meanwhile, my one brother had been struggling mightily with his own mental health since my mom died. He received his medical services through the Veterans Administration. You know the agency, my Kindreds, the same one that had botched my step-dad's surgery. They were another broken part of our system. The hoops he had to jump through to try and get seen were mind-boggling. At his lowest, he tried to seek inpatient help. He was turned away because they had no open beds. Again, my Kindreds, I will ask you: why is this acceptable? If someone is desperate enough to seek mental health resources – limited as they already are – why is it an acceptable practice to turn people away? Then all the mental health professionals will rue the suicide rate, while actually not doing much to prevent it. It is insanity in itself.

None of these recent events did anything to soothe my disturbed psyche. Angelica didn't stay long and was moving in with a girlfriend until she figured out what to do next. When she left, my brother moved in. It was a constantly revolving door. I was just grateful I could help those I loved. It gave me a much -needed self-confidence boost.

Fall arrived in a riot of colors that perked my spirits somewhat. Optimism was a foreign concept to me for the first time in my life. I was typically the cheerleader - the yes man, or woman, more accurately. My whole life, I existed to be the helper. I was the oldest of four, so it was ingrained in me. That is not to say I disliked my role, quite the opposite, actually. Most of my fulfillment was directly correlated to others' fulfillment. It was co-dependence at its best. I realized it, but was helpless to change it. Until I broke, that is.

There were some offers on my mom's place, but most were low ball, and some downright insulting. My step dad was hard to deal with on a good day, so I was the go-between for him and the real estate agent. She was a sweetheart that we had used before. I was not opening her up to any of the negativity that seemed constant. Yes, I readily admit again that I struggled with the boundary thing. I honestly could have handled the majority of it alone, but I didn't want anyone to think I was getting anything out of this. That was a point of pride for me. I was doing it so that I could have a clean conscience moving forward and not be tethered to anyone. That may sound harsh, but it was self-care. I hadn't had a relationship with his people in the 30-something years our parents had been married. Why would I want to now? Many phone calls were going back and forth about what to do for my stepdad's care. Even when I called to talk about the sale, it always devolved into that topic. My mom's husband couldn't handle much of anything, it seemed.

My ma had paid all the bills, done all the cooking, cleaning, and errands —plus, his tube feedings, and grinding his meds. Jocelyn, a nurse, had sent Mom an actual pestle and mortar. This was a grueling routine that had led to my mother's demise. I wanted no parts of it.

"I am handling the sale of his house so that he has money to pay for his care" was my standard line when they called.

That was not the answer they wanted. The phone calls continued. I had taken to calling them "The Bullshit Carousel," and happily, neither voice in my head objected. I take my wins where I can get them nowadays.

It seemed his kids weren't cool with him spending all of his money on his care. I guess they wanted an inheritance or something. As it stood, both of our parents had been barely making it. Hence, the reason my mom didn't want to go to the hospital was. They both had to retire early due to health conditions, and had both worked for the newspapers. They ended up robbed of pension money when it all collapsed due to the rise of digital literacy. I was unsure what they expected me to do about any of this. What mattered to me, I already had: cookbooks, pictures, decorations, baking pans, and of course, her jewelry. I shared all of this with my family. It was what she would have wanted.

When the house finally sold, a weight lifted. As Robert Frost said, though, I had "miles to go before I sleep."

Chapter 10

With the sale and clean out of my mom's place done, I had expected to feel whole again. I didn't. Driving back to Delco the night of the sale, the sun was setting, and the clouds were crazy beautiful. They looked like angel wings - they were in decipherable shapes, with all the ends of the clouds turning into wisps that resembled feathers. Maybe I was reaching, but it felt like a sign from my mom that she was alright. She was telling me I did well. I waited for the ache to recede.

Yet, it felt like that house was my last tie to my Mom. I drove by it to make sure it was being cared for. Life moved on. The world moved on. Or perhaps it didn't. The war in Ukraine raged on. Both major parties continued to call for investigations of the opposing side, not caring that this was a major waste of taxpayer money. Nor did our elected officials seem to care about the things that really mattered: inflation, education, health care, crime – I could go on. Even in my fractured mental state, I could detect the pattern: those in places of power (politicians, administrators) collected large sums of money for not doing their job.

In fact, they were doing the opposite of what was needed. Inaction and distraction were now the law of the land, it seemed. I avoided watching the news because it only served to depress me further. My GI issues began to relent after the sale went through, and that was most definitely a positive. Once again, things began to settle.

It was aforementioned, though, that I always approached these times with fearful hope. I held my breath, cautiously optimistic, always waiting for the other shoe to drop. I have read a lot of self-care books, blogs, and articles over the years. I knew that what you put out into the universe tends to find its way back to you. It wasn't lost on me that I put out a lot more negativity than I ever had. That was another big reason I stayed home; I had nothing positive to contribute to conversations, situations, and the like.

As my mom always said, "If you have nothing nice to say, say nothing at all."

Personally, I preferred Olympia Dukakis' response in *Steel Magnolias*: "If you have nothing nice to say, come sit next to me." My Cinematic Tourette's is showing itself again.

This time, though, it wasn't a shoe that dropped; rather, it was a tree. On my cabin. We had just put on a new roof, not even a year ago. We hoped like hell it didn't leak.

Our homeowner's insurance company was really helpful and had an adjuster out quickly. We were cut a check to pay the roofers to fix it. There were pieces of this huge tree all over. We cleaned up what we reasonably could and waited. It took quite some time to order the materials and set up an install. When the order arrived, they sent the wrong color. Again, we waited.

Meanwhile, the roof did indeed leak all down the walls and ceiling beams. The wood was beginning to swell, and we were disgusted. Just one more thing that went wrong at the absolute worst time. I made a mental note to fix it in the spring. About two months later, the roof was fixed, and with the correct color. While we were just grateful it was done, it had definitely been another layer to the stress onion that neither of us needed.

One of our largest issues as a family, besides the rampant mental illness we now all live with, was that when I went on Long Term Disability, Aaron lost his benefits, because I had carried the family. My contract year ends on July 1st. After that, he was on his own.

Fortunately, Tony and Ella hopped on their company's benefits, but Aaron, being a delivery driver, did not. It was currently the only job he could handle. He needed something where he didn't have to interact with anyone. He busted his butt doing it- sometimes working up to 70 hours a week, but health care remained elusive. It's funny how people think you just jump on Obamacare, but for a single person working, the cost was prohibitive.

We had filled out an application for state insurance and for social security insurance during the summer. It took us forever – we were sharing the same defunct brain space. Neither of us had our wits about us, and we both knew it. Aaron and I were still struggling mightily, and we forged a friendship through it. We came up with catchy little optimistic slogans to throw at each other during the dark days. Other times, we sat in complete silence, neither feeling the need to fill it with drivel.

Another symptom of my madness was loud noises. I could not suffer them anymore. This was especially problematic since I lived with the loudest people known to man. When my kids were little, they loved that Disney show *The Proud Family*. I have always joked that we were "The Loud Family." Most days were fine since my family was at work. It was when they got home, the circus started. Many nights, I just went to bed rather than implore them to take it down a notch.

On those nights, I lay in bed awake, wondering when my mental condition would improve. I missed the old me – optimistic, funny, sarcastic, and together. I had always organized everything, both at work and at home. Now I couldn't organize a meal to cook for my family. There was very little grace in my headspace. I beat myself up, and replayed everything negative in my head over and over.

"You will never be you again," stated the negative one. "She died when your mother did." For once, I couldn't disagree.

With the holidays swiftly approaching, one would think I would be throwing myself into holiday prep. Typically, I would. I was my mother's daughter. Baking would usually begin in November and then be frozen for my cookie giveaway. That was my way of spreading holiday cheer. I would make cookie bags for neighbors, friends, family, and of course, my students. Baking would have been a nice distraction if only I could get myself together.

That year had been a roller-coaster ride straight to hell, and I still resided there. Tony was on call for work this Thanksgiving, so we decided to stay home and host. It would be us, the kids, my brother, that was living with us, and my youngest brother and his wife. Intimate and low-key. We were all missing my mom, so it would be nice to be together. I went through the motions – purchase turkey, stuffing, and all the trimmings. I actually made a few pies, but there wasn't any joy in it like there would have been.

Without the anticipation of having everyone together – my mom included – the season just didn't mean as much. There had been a scant few holidays that she and I weren't together. We would be on the phone the night before Thanksgiving, with me having just finished parent-teacher conferences. I was exhausted but happy that the holidays were upon us, and excited to share them with my loved ones.

As mentioned before, Kindreds, my mom was a spectacular cook. She and I would plan the menu and split it up. That allowed us to have a veritable feast! I can almost smell it. On this Thanksgiving morning, I got up early to put the turkey in. My move was usually to make coffee and watch the Philly parade on TV, covered in a blanket until it was time to baste.

As children and teens, we always went to the parade with my mom. Some years, we would do New Year's at the Mummers Parade instead of Thanksgiving. That is one of the great joys of being from Philly or Delco. We know how to do a parade right.

Other years, I was in the parade with either my mom or my friend Kacey's mom.

One time, my mom dressed as a clown for the Children's Hospital along with my niece and Angelica. They had a blast. I missed those simple days so much. Life is too difficult and dark nowadays.

Anyhow, I am watching the parade, remembering all of this, crying. Sometimes, a walk down Memory Lane is not what you need. My heart felt as if it were literally breaking in my chest. I could feel it wrenching, and my stomach took up the symphony. I hoped for a massive heart attack like my dad had. At least that was quick, even if not painless.

Unfortunately, all I did was spend the day between the bathroom and the kitchen. Appetizing, yes? My hands were raw from scrubbing pots, pans, and China after washing them a zillion times while using the bathroom.

My youngest brother and his wife contracted COVID and couldn't come. Jocelyn and her family stopped by with desserts. I couldn't even get off the couch. They didn't stay.

"You chased away what little family you have left," spat the negative one, "doesn't matter. You will die alone anyhow."

"Don't we all?" quipped my inner monologue. I smirked and headed to bed.

My whole-body hurts. I know that is common with depression, but this was otherworldly. My back was singing in pain, and my knees burned, a low, slow fire that never completely dissipated. Add in that GI issues were making a return along with the debut of the holidays, and I was a hurt piece. I didn't dare drive, especially with my grandson in the car. It's funny how you know your limits, even when you don't know anything else.

As it were, I ordered everything for Christmas online in one day. It was the last day to receive guaranteed delivery before the holiday.

"Well, at least you pulled that part off," mused my inner monologue.

"Good luck wrapping it all," Negative Nelly piped up.

"Tony will," I said, lifting both middle fingers skyward.

And he did. God bless my husband.

"He is the best of the best. Forget all the rest," I chanted to myself, as I set about the task of baking. This particular gem was a throwback from my cheerleading days.

Lately, I have resorted to living in the past. As mentioned, there are many unaccounted-for, lost hours during my year in hell. Or maybe it was Limbo. I hear the Catholic Church doesn't subscribe to that anymore. I wouldn't know.

This was different, though. It wasn't like the lost hours I experienced after I had to stay out of work. These hours weren't lost at all – they were found. I wandered down the pathways of my psyche as I carried out daily routines. I remembered the Halloween costumes my mom always hand-sewed and our decorated bikes, which we used to ride in the 4th of July parades as children. Camping trips, amusement parks, the beach —it was all still right there for the picking if you had the time, which was currently at a premium.

It was comforting to dwell on the people and events from the past that I hadn't thought about in years. The memories were like dusty little diamonds taken off the shelf of my psyche. I was eager to examine them. In depth. For hours. Because it felt like home.

Chapter 11

The soundtrack of my mind had started up again. Usually, it was Christmas tunes in December, but not this year. Several times, I awoke to Oasis' "Don't Look Back In Anger" being played in my brain, just for me to hear. I suppose one could say this signaled the anger phase of grieving for me, Kindreds. I remember reading the quote from C.S. Lewis saying, "I sat with my anger long enough until she told me her real name was grief." Certainly, they seem to go hand in hand.

According to Elisabeth Kubler-Ross in her book *On Death and Dying* (1969), the stages of grief are non-linear and can happen in any particular order. Kubler-Ross cites these stages as: denial, anger, bargaining, depression, and acceptance.

"Alright, well, you already have depression, so maybe we can skip that?" asked my inner voice innocently.

It was almost as if she were baiting the negative one. As we all know, negative breeds negative, so she surely made an appearance.

"Maybe we skip," said the negative one - mimicking the sweet, singsong cadence that my inner voice used sometimes to soothe me – "All of them!" she roared.

Then, it was quiet once more. Her words hung in my head like a bell that echoes softly through the wind. Even when the breeze stopped, I could still hear the chiming, far, far away. She was right, I thought. Lately, I could feel the slide.

That's another fallacy of depression – that we just sink in, unaware of how deep we are. As Sylvia Path declared, "I am aware. Catastrophically aware." You see, the truth is much more diabolical: We know that we are sunk and we are helpless to pull ourselves out.

It's much like the meme about quicksand. I was slugging through that every day, carrying the baggage of a hundred lifetimes, it felt like.

Therefore, people suffering from the particular mix I have going tend to berate themselves about all the things they can't do or handle. In turn, we cycle deeper down into the darkness. It's a hamster wheel of torture and dysfunction for sure. I do not recommend. Zero stars.

Seriously, though, with Christmas upon us, I felt like I was at rock bottom again. I prayed it was just the holidays and not a real regression. Admittedly, I was nearing suicidal, but I wouldn't tell anyone until it passed. And it would. I hoped. I prayed.

It is worth mentioning that even when I was feeling that way, I was aware of it. I was an active agent in my own future in a way I never had been before. This basically equated to the lure of that poisonous moss and the gleam of the blade. How would it end?

One afternoon, coming home from the cabin shortly before Christmas, the sun was waning, and the woods on the side of the highway looked so inviting. There were thick, lush pines that usually would have me thinking of Christmas, as their aroma bled through the heating vents of the car. No gingerbread visions were dancing in my head, though.

Instead of warm, cozy Christmas thoughts, this beckoned to me. I closed my eyes and imagined how wonderful it would feel to just lie down in the bed of shed pine needles and gaze up at the starry sky while it darkened. I don't know if the English language, or any language for that matter, has a word for this. I just wanted to lie down right there in that forest and call it a day. Or a life. The need to do this was so strong that the muscles in my legs were twitching and jumping painfully. I shifted constantly in my seat as Tony drove. Once again, I thought of the Robert Frost poem.

The woods are lovely, dark and deep,
But I have promises to keep,

Honestly, I credit my grandson and the old Catholic ways for making me hold on. Kaleb had his whole life ahead of him, and I didn't want just to be a memory. It was bad enough that my mom was. As for the Catholic thing, well, I certainly didn't identify with them anymore, but I was definitely a Christian, and suicide was not looked kindly on. It wasn't in any religion that I was aware of, except for extremists. So, I hung on, hoping for better days.

Since all the hours of the past year were a blur, so were those leading up to Christmas. The days I remembered most were those in wherein I had a panic attack. Oh yes – I was back to that, Kindreds.

For the first time in my life, I wanted to say "eff off Christmas," and not celebrate, but I had a grandchild now. He was coming to the cabin for Christmas, along with my offspring and my brother. So I pushed through, getting all the food, alcohol, gift wrap, and trimmings. If I planned on making it through the holidays, I sensed I was in need of a medication increase. This made me more despondent, because I wanted off the meds, not an increase. Yet, I recognized that I was living in the dark and struggling to find my way to the light.

At this point, I was no longer really drinking. The meds changes had wreaked absolute havoc on my system, in addition to the physical effects the holidays were having on me. I had re-visited the side of a mountain road, vomiting, pooping, and panic-attacking. Food wasn't appetizing anymore, so I only ate enough to get by. I puked most of everything up. Finally, I could no longer hold my alcohol.

This was difficult, given that it was my crutch of choice, as I have stated previously. However, the damage was too great with the new meds I was taking. I could have one or two tops if I watered my drink down. This is big for a functioning alcoholic such as myself. Truth be, I wasn't even functioning, but you get the picture. Alcohol was my go-to, and now it was forbidden.

Christmas came, and I made it until dinner, and then I couldn't finish. I went and lay in my bedroom, crying. Tony offered to finish it for me. I agreed and cried myself to sleep. I felt a little better the next day, and then by the time we headed home, the panic attacks were once more in the rearview.

We entertained for New Year's – another holiday usually spent with my mom. Our town in Delco does some truly cool stuff for the holiday season. We had hoped to take Kaleb up the main drag, but after dinner, all I wanted to do was chill. My brother and Kellie banged pots and pans at midnight, while the rest of us watched from the warmth of the house.

"Good riddance," I thought to myself.

After New Year's, it was sort of like a switch flipped. I started to come out of it again. The GI issues abated, and the anxiety was manageable. I had messaged Dr. Merry in mid- December, when things started to get really awful.

Unfortunately, she was now out on medical leave, and I was assigned a young woman who did not deal with Long Term Disability, and she informed me of that right up front. I respected her honesty, but was dismayed. I fought to find a kindred soul, and now she was gone too, even if temporarily. We had vibed so well. We ended our November session talking about Thanksgiving plans. I held Dr. Merry in such high esteem and prayed she would get better. I worried, and that's part of my anxiety, and part of my heart.

This new woman suggested a med in addition to the regular one if I was considering going back to work. LTD came calling at the beginning of January because it had been a calendar year since I was out of work, collecting benefits. I only made 60% of my income, and everything Tony and I had managed to save was gone, and all the credit cards we had recently paid off were maxed again. It was time.

Tina and I met in person to fill out the paperwork. The case manager informed me that I could be sent back with accommodations. This seemed the best route to me, and Tina agreed. I loved and respected Tina. She was one of my tribe: people who care about me and support me. Dr. Merry was one, too. As were my family and friends. My circle may be shrinking, but it is still mighty.

We worked together, at her office, to muddle through yet another mountain of paperwork. I was beyond grateful for the help and guidance again. Tina took the time to ask my opinion and helped me weigh the pros and cons. These were pretty simple cognitive abilities that I just currently don't possess.

Our list of accommodations was simple, but thorough. We asked that I be given a guaranteed prep time each day, since teachers were still losing theirs. We also cited the need for a no-sub clause, three days to clean out my classroom and prepare it for students, and a meeting with my principal.

There had been an open war through email about the preps. Not only were teachers losing them, but accounts payable was slacking on paying for these lost preps. They screwed the teachers in December – right before Christmas – of their prep money. I was unsure if it was due to chronic dysfunction or a little last-minute punishment. People were bitter, and rightfully so. Either way, I wanted no part of it.

"A little too late," soothed my inner voice.

Breathlessly, I waited for the other. Thankfully, she missed her chance to make me feel like total and complete crap again because I wasn't good enough at that all on my own, like I needed her help in that department.

Since subbing had been the proverbial straw that broke this camel's back, it was a hard line I was drawing. Plus, my room had raw sewage in it the last time I had been in there. I realized it was cleaned up because the school store was being run out of there, but I knew all the bookcases on the floor could be damaged.

Add in that I had brought roaches home with me in a box of books I needed to teach with during the pandemic, and I figured the classroom was overrun again since it was a dumping ground whenever I wasn't there. Obviously, my little classroom sanctuary needed an overhaul! You better bet that the morons in administration were giving me paid time to do it.

Also, since my principal was lazy and relied on fake friendship and charm to get by, I wanted a meeting to ensure he was crystal clear on all of it. I also wanted to resign from my positions for PBIS, MTSS, and Student Council. I was getting in there, doing my job, and getting back out —no more extras, no more anything other than giving my little tribe of students their best seven.

My administration had taxed me to my limits, all while preaching self- care. They used me up and then threw me to the wolves. My principal was never held accountable for the damage done while I was out burying my mother. Until now, that is. There were some things I could forgive, but I will never forget. He needed to know all of this if I were coming back to reside in peace. Even if I were only there temporarily- which I openly hoped was the case. I wanted out for good after this year.

Chapter 12

February was upon us. My return date loomed large in all our minds. Angelica would have to change her work schedule so I could still watch Kaleb. Aaron was still experiencing symptoms of his illness that would not abate with the medication. I suspected he needed an increase, like I had done, but he was still without health insurance. We had a phone hearing the previous week with a judge and a representative for Social Security.

They claimed not to have received a single page of the 199 pages of tax documents I had faxed them for Aaron. As such, it was continued, and we had two days to find that one paper and get it to them, which we did. Now they were claiming it went to the wrong place.

Apparently, the Bullshit Carousel was a ride I couldn't get off of. I had a lifetime ticket. We called yet again. Aaron and I had the agent on speaker phone. He was now claiming Aaron hadn't had a hearing at all, after leaving us on hold for an hour. I took over the conversation, and I was hot. I informed him that there indeed was a hearing, and I had been on the phone with him for it. All of a sudden, his tone changed.

"And who are you, I might ask?" he inquired.

"This is Aaron's mom," I answered, the hostility dripping from my voice. "I help him with all of this since he has a disability, and you guys just constantly give him the runaround." There was no disguising my extreme anger and frustration.

As he suddenly decides he can "dig deeper," I intentionally remark to Aaron that I had never sympathized with the Unabomber until now.

"Excuse me, ma'am, but are you threatening me?" he asked icily.

"I am talking to my son, not to you," I spat back. He piped down.

There were zero answers from this idiot, and I disconnected. Ella was right – why did life have to be so hard anymore? I still had no answers on any level. The amount of hoops we were expected to jump through just to get something he was legally entitled to was crazy in itself. I fully realized that the government hoped I would give up. Lord knows I felt like it.

Meanwhile, Aaron was getting worse instead of better. I had been able to secure him three months' worth of meds from the pharmaceutical company that makes them. This "free" program they run took over two months to get. You are supposed to receive an answer within 72 hours of applying. The back and forth with them —sending tax documents, doctor's notes, and people losing them — was a trend, it seemed. I thought, and not for the first time, how weird life is since the pandemic. I despise the phrase the "new normal," but I fear that's exactly what this is. No one seems to do their job well anymore, and people are not held accountable for it. The world was just a giant ball of filthy yarn that would never be untangled. It made me long to leave again.

When I speak of jumping through unnecessary hoops, that is to say, this was not isolated to one or two events. This strange, dispiriting phenomenon blanketed everything. Lost paperwork, tax information, emails, faxes, portals, unrecognized credentials, phone calls, wait times, wrong answers only, and waiting for a call back that never came. I could go on and on.

It literally felt like the universe was fighting me every step of the way. My feet encased in concrete was the vision I kept getting. All I had to do was jump off the bridge and peacefully allow myself to sink. Yet, I couldn't bring myself to do it. I have explained my reasons, and they haven't changed.

Back in February of last year, when my mom died, I had gone online to pay my taxes. We owed, which was infuriating, but once again, Kindreds – another topic for another day.

Anyhow, I paid them and didn't realize I had to choose a tax year to apply it to. Why it wouldn't just be applied to my amount due is beyond me, especially since the payment was for the same amount owed, but I digress.

Since my mind was so broken when my mom died, I didn't realize I had already paid them, and I set up a payment plan. I paid the other half of what I had previously paid. Dumb, I know.

By the time I figured this out, they had sent a letter detailing how they were set to garnish Tony's wages. Biden had hired thousands and thousands of tax agents! What were they all doing? How did this keep falling through the cracks? I had wasted umpteen hours on hold and speaking to various agents. Wait times could exceed three hours —my Bullshit Carousel. Apparently, there is way more than one driver .... only one lonely rider though. The IRS assured me no garnishment would take place.

If you guessed that the IRS garnished Tony's wages anyhow, you would again be correct, Kindreds. Cue up the constant Bullshit Carousel, even though I have motion sickness. That is yet another hell unto itself: no rides, no boats, no back seats of cars. As travelers with my parents when we were young, I was always sick the first couple of days of vacation. It sucks because planes are difficult too. Tony always says that I give a watermelon and he needs a seed. That is what writers do, though. It's also what I do at work. I ask students for a seed (topic) and we develop it into a watermelon (essay).

Alas, much like my dealings with the state insurance, each IRS agent told me something different. It was beyond frustrating and demoralizing. Our government was so broken. Just like our world, my work, my family, and myself.

There were just too many negatives stacking up. I could feel the precipice of the abyss lurking over my shoulder. I realize now that I will spend the rest of my life glancing back to make sure I am safe. That's trauma. I have studied enough of it to earn my Master's and have consistently chosen trauma-informed teaching as my topic for our required yearly read. So many of my students needed this. Now I did, too.

Paranoia had led me not to leave the house. Of course, the GI issues, meds, and all that were another matter. During the darkest days, when I did try and force myself out of my comfort zone, the paranoia was too great.

One time at lunch with my cousin Jocelyn and her mom, I insisted at the man at the table behind us was a spy for my school district and was recording us.

"The admin will say if she is good enough to go to lunch, she is good enough to come to work," I told her while my aunt was in the bathroom.

Jocelyn leaned in close and said in a soft voice, "Jen, you gotta stop."

But I couldn't, and that was the rub. Thankfully, this abated with time. It is pure hell to have an anxiety disorder already so severe wherein you are experiencing panic attacks, pooping and puking, but let's throw on paralyzing paranoia.

"Paranoia will destroy ya," my inner voice sang out. She enjoyed my Cinematic Tourette's, even when it spread to songs.

"Good thing you saved all the pills," the negative one baited. "You may still need them. I mean, you may be off all but two now, but think of the bottle upon bottle, just sitting in the closet for the taking," she pushed.

"God forbid any progress be made...." I started the inner voice, and I cut her off.

For the first time in quite a while, I pushed right back at that beastly bitch, with my full-on, authentic voice.

"I didn't survive the past year just to cop out now," I said firmly.

The ensuing quiet was uncomfortable. I sat with it, waiting. Nothing. I had succeeded in shutting them both up for now.

While I was making small strides towards healing, Aaron was sinking deeper into his illness. His eyes were starting to look wild again. He claimed to still be taking the meds I had fought to get him. If he indeed was taking them, he needed a med increase or a n overhaul. It was obvious they weren't helping him anymore. An entire year had passed since Aaron was able to see a psychiatrist or a therapist due to his lack of health care. The government had us chasing our tails, just as they wanted.

Once again, inaction and ineptness ruled the day. I can't stress enough that I felt like a failure as his mom. Nothing I did seemed to help. We were getting nowhere. His medication was in excess of $1600.00 monthly. Who could afford that?

He had pulled a knife on his roommate after my mom had passed, when he was deep in despair. Even though they were basically close friends since infancy, his roomie was not having it. Could I blame him? Absolutely not. Mental illness ends friendships and decimates families. Jocelyn was a nurse. She found some resources for free legal aid to help in our dealings with SSI. We were beyond grateful, especially since it felt as if the world was against us. I helped him fill out the application, and he was given an appointment. I prayed this was the answer.

One morning, shortly after I was trying to have my coffee, I decided to switch on the news. The news anchor was discussing the mess at the border. Some southern governors were now shipping immigrants to other states, as they could not handle the influx. I watched as the video clips showed non-Americans receiving health care services free of charge.

Now, I have nothing against immigrants being given health care, but what about my son? We have lived here our entire lives, paid ridiculous amounts in taxes, yet because of his demographics, he couldn't get a damn thing. The injustice of it roiled my innards. We are a nation founded on immigrants. I understand this. Yet, how about the average Joe? You know the one carrying the load?

Why did I ever think watching network news was a good idea? I quickly switched off the television, proud of myself for finding the remote on the first try. It's those little things that keep me going, Kindreds.

In regard to my return to work, that was going over like a lead balloon. The assigned vocational counselor couldn't get in touch with anyone from my work. Shocker, eh? I gave him what little info I had and hoped for the best. That is what my life had become: wishing and hoping. It felt as if everything was out of my control. I suppose it is.

As the days passed by, the new Jen began to emerge. Gone were the days of worrying needlessly, helicopter parenting, and bitterness. I would help where I could, and the rest? Well, let's just say that I had come to a level of acceptance with everything, which gave me much-needed peace. I accepted that I can't change the world, that I was just a helpless pawn in a much bigger game. I accepted that my kids weren't perfect, and as adults, they had to make their own decisions, come hell or high water. All I could do was pick up the pieces afterwards. I would dispense advice only when asked, because unsolicited advice is basically just criticism.

I began to develop non-inflammatory responses to my children's insanity. This served to protect my peace as well as my relationship with them. Ella had been a support system throughout this entire ordeal.

Even so, she was out of patience with the constant negatives. Her car accident had taken months to resolve. Our experience with the insurance agencies was similar to that of the government. No answers, no call backs, just dodging responsibility. This is a post-pandemic phenomenon that irks me to no end. I have spoken on the lack of accountability and initiative on every level. No wonder my beloved US was in such a mess.

Always eager to help, I assisted her in contacting the Pennsylvania Insurance Commission, another government entity, and my Kindreds. I assure you; they were no different. There was no help to be had, and she suffered a loss on her car.

Another post-pandemic issue no one is addressing is the lack of affordable housing and vehicles. We found a car she could afford, and the transmission died on the way home. Unbelievable, right?

Like I have said before, I have a lifetime ticket to ride the Bullshit Carousel. Ensuing phone calls, emails, and battles began. The man who sold her the car was telling us to "piss off." I was not giving in. No one was ripping my kid off her hard-earned money. We reached out to anyone we thought could help us, but of course, no one could.

In the end, Tony and I lent her the money to fix it. I wrote negative reviews of the place that had sold her a lemon on every social outlet I could.

There was little satisfaction, though. She had it for about 6 months when someone hit her as she was parked in the local Wawa parking lot. Once again, months went by with no resolution. We pestered and badgered them to do their job and fix the vehicle. They didn't. They totaled it. Even though it was only a taillight and quarter panel, she had been driving it with no issues, but it just wouldn't pass inspection like that. So here we were back to square one.

Her frustration and angst were palpable, and I shared it. Yes, life gives you lemons.

My ability to mix those lemons with some vodka and muster on was still stripped from me. The GI issues cropped up now and then, but thankfully, they seemed mostly under control.

"Another reason to be grateful," my inner voice reminded me.

Lately, the negative one has been mostly quiet. I didn't need my inner voice to remind me to be grateful for that! What I have been discovering is that the more I leaned towards peace, the less she appeared. That was my self-care now, peace. If it didn't flow or vibe, I was walking away.

Of course, there were situations I couldn't just quit. Examples include work and my family. Aaron was progressively getting worse. One night, he attacked Ella. He was black out drunk and choked her. Not once, but three times. The last time, she couldn't break free. Her boyfriend had to pull Aaron off her. She came home with bruises and scratches on her neck. Her man was lumped up, too. He didn't want to hit Aaron because he was also friends with him.

Needless to say, it was an awful situation. Ella and Aaron were only two years apart and super close. This drove a wedge into their relationship that I feared wouldn't go away. Now, Aaron was down another friend and family member.

That is not to say that I am condoning his behavior at all. I was horrified, as was Tony. In fact, I told Tony he had to take the reins on this one. Nothing I had done for Aaron in the past year had deterred him from resorting to violence. It was time for Dad to step in.

This was absolutely the right move, and one the old Jen never would have made. The former me would have preferred to drown rather than ask for help. Part of that was pride, and part was stubbornness. The rest of it was the fact that I had always been large and in charge. I liked helping. I craved it. I had always been a problem solver. A mover and a shaker. This had always been my role, until it no longer could be.

Nevertheless, my mental breakdown had taken me to places I didn't care to revisit. I accepted – possibly for the first time in my 52 years – that I couldn't fix everything, no matter how hard I tried. I had to let go and let God. As I mentioned, I am a woman of prayer –I still pray every night in bed. I always have, although the intentions change. Now it was all Aaron. I prayed every evening that he would hold on until we could get him the help he needed and deserved.

Although I understood his desire to drown out the voices with alcohol, it was a crutch he could not pick up. Aaron had a liver disorder that did not allow his body to break down alcohol properly. Further, he had a brain aneurysm that had gone unchecked since he had no insurance. My kid was a walking time bomb.

Some days, I had to take the new emergency meds to be able to deal with him. He was never difficult as a child. In fact, Aaron was the most copacetic baby and child I had ever seen. The ways in which this illness had changed him were horrendous. He had alienated most of his friends and Ella. He was alone most of the time anymore. The only times he wasn't were if he came to our house or if his roommate was home.

What's worse, the voices were reminding him of his singularity. One day, he told me that a female's voice distinctly said to him while he was brushing his teeth that morning, "He was utterly and totally alone."

Imagine if you will the horror of that for a moment, Kindreds. His roommate is a guy, and he was at work. There was literally no one home but Aaron. I can't imagine how scared he must have been, especially given his current state. My heart broke when he told me, and I was surprised there was anything left intact to break. Life just continued to suck in perpetuity.

Our one shining light was Kaleb. I clung to him like a life vest. He gave me so much joy, this beautiful, sweet little boy. He loved to snuggle and be sung to, just as my babies had. I splurged and bought myself the first thing I had purchased just for me in years – a pink rocker. I loved it and so did he.

It truly soothed my sore soul to rock and hum to him as he fell asleep in my arms. Some days, I would just sit holding him after he nodded off, enjoying the feel of his solid little body snuggled up against me. I wanted to protect him so badly from all of the awful in the world. I remembered back to wanting the same for my own, and we see how that turned out.

Possibly the most dreadful part of all was the fact that Aaron at first thought that Ella and her boyfriend must have attacked each other. He could not for a minute even entertain the idea that he had done that to his little sister. His mind was paranoia-driven, so it made sense to him that another family member would be setting him up for a fall.

It was incomprehensible to me that he actually believed that, but I chose acceptance and peace. He, of course, had a price to pay for what he had done. We just had to wait it out until he realized that. To say it was awkward when Aaron came over and Ella was home would be an understatement. I tried my best to be supportive, especially of Ella. She had cried for days after it happened.

"Mom, never in my worst nightmares did I think my brother was capable of that," she sobbed.

As terrible as I felt, I was hopeless to change any of this, but I accepted it. This general acceptance of it all was what brought me back from the brink. I hated that I was so powerless, but there were too many fights to win them all. This is self-care. I accept that there are things I cannot change, no matter how hard I try. I acknowledge this and keep on fighting the good fight. That's all I got.

Chapter 13

The soundtrack of my mind was back, and this time, I awoke to an old hymn from my childhood. It was always one of my favorites. My dad's name is Francis, so "Make Me an Instrument of Your Peace" has special meaning to me. Plus, St. Francis was an avid animal lover, just like me. I hadn't thought about my father in a long time. Everything was my mom lately since I was missing her terribly. It was still difficult to come to terms with the fact that they were both gone now, even though he had been dead for over 30 years.

"Old wounds never truly heal," observed my inner voice.

Perhaps it was the hymn, or the prayers, maybe it was my mindset, but the negative one remained at bay. I was thankful and acknowledged it.

When I spoke to Tina about our situation, she was equally horrified. She had been rooting for Aaron. Plus, she knew how devastating this was to us. She validated my fears that the family dynamic could forever remain off now. Tina was damn good at what she did, and I was grateful for her.

"So we know he isn't in a full-blown crisis yet," she stated. "But the spiral down towards that is obvious."

I knew she was preparing me for the inevitable onset of another major mental fracture for Aaron.

"Until he can take responsibility for his actions, there really isn't any growth or forgiveness. Nor any moving forward. For anyone," she sagely stated. I knew this to be true.

"Unfortunately, I can't force him to think rationally, Tina," I lamented.

She understood. She also knew that there were no easy answers. I liked that Tina didn't even try and sugar coat things for me. She was a realist —much like me. Her best approach was to help me build an arsenal of non-inflammatory responses to the daily crazy I dealt with. She helped me to develop healthy coping strategies and pushed me to draw boundaries with my family and work.

In fact, she applauded me for turning the most recent Aaron debacle over to Tony. She knew full well I was trying to break the lifelong habit of over achieving and pleasing people.

Speaking of which, my step father had been calling. I hadn't made time to return his call. So, he resorted to phoning Angelica. Once she told me, I knew I had to give in and call back. There was no way I wanted him bothering my children. When I finally got in touch with him, it was the usual. Complaints and updates. Now that my mom was gone, he had suddenly decided to take an interest in his health — too late, if you ask me.

For years, he had defied everything he was told because he didn't like the answers he was being given. Well, guess what, Kindreds? None of us like the answers most time.

Yet, to make life more difficult for the only person who cared enough to take care of your sorry ass was inexcusable in my eyes. I am just going to come right out and say it: I hold him responsible for my mom's decline. It is the one thing that I can't forgive. She had so much more to offer the world. What did he have? Negativity. I will never in my life accept that she is six feet under while he still walks this earth. It is my one and only that I will n ever come to terms with.

Just because life is grossly unjust does not mean I have to swallow it. Swallow it, I did, though, when conversing with him. There was no desire to argue with him, or even to put him in his place. He was a lost cause and always had been. It's impossible to change after 70 years of patriarchal attitudes and actions.

Thus far, I have been able to hold my tongue. Naturally, that could change at any moment. After I heard what his request was, I didn't bother to. He wanted to fly up here from Florida for the one-year anniversary of my mom's death. Further, he wanted all of us to go to the cemetery with him.

Now this may seem like a really nice thought or gesture. However, one must know him to realize that this was all a charade. What he really wanted was to be the center of attention. He craved the drama of standing around her grave with her kids and grandkids and crying how much he loved her. He wanted to be a show piece of grief and then collapse. He wanted to be helped to the car and mooned over.

This was another conversation Tina applauded me for.

"Absolutely not," I told him point-blank. "I go there every month by myself to make sure it is being cared for. I can't handle going there with a group of people."

As usual, he wouldn't take "no" for an answer.

"But I think being together for this is important. I know it would be important to your mother," he attempted to reason.

"Ah, there it is," said my inner voice. She was right, of course. He was not above resorting to guilt to get his way.

What he failed to realize, though, was that I had none. I did right by my ma. Always had for the most part. I was heartbroken and empty, but certainly not guilty of anything other than overextending myself. This man was not someone that I was willing to do that for. There were precious few of them anymore, to be honest. It was another way I had changed.

Although I honestly never had the time for him. He made his entrance into our house particularly painful. He was physically abusive to my brother, the one living with me. I had no doubt this was part of my bro's mental problems. I spoke up, of course, and my brother once told me he hated when I had sleepovers as a teen, because it was always worse then. Even when I thought I was helping fix the situation, he outfoxed me. I was green back then and naïve. I am neither now.

"Mom knows I go there. I cry every time, and I am still having a hard time handling it. I am not willing to open myself up to more drama." My voice was firm. I did not stutter.

Again, he tried, but I cut him off.

"It's a hard no," I told him firmly, "I am drawing that boundary and sticking to it. Why don't you call your son? Plan it with him," I suggested.

My youngest brother was only six when our dad died. My step father had adopted him a few years later. Many times over the years, I have told my step dad that I have a father who raised me. I had just turned eighteen when my dad passed. I did not need a father, or even a father figure.

While I listened to him complain, I realized that he had no idea how my mom's death had affected anyone but him. Nor did I believe he truly cared how anyone was coping. It was all about him. He made small talk and politely inquired after the kids and Kaleb. So, I decided to let him know exactly what was up. I didn't gloss over anything; I gave him the real, raw, ugly version of my life currently.

"Let him see he isn't the only one who has it bad," my inner voice soothed.

"Let him have it!" the negative one screeched.

Of course, she made herself heard. Why wouldn't she seize the opportunity? I mean, I was on the phone with the man who oozed negativity out of every pore.

Fortunately, this seemed to work, and he let me hang up sooner rather than later. I realized I was onto something and vowed just to unload every time he called, and maybe eventually he would leave me alone. It's all I wanted. To be left alone.

At the end of January, a friend reached out. She had seen some posts from a Facebook page that she belonged to and wanted to know what I thought. I went onto the social media site to see what was up. A school board member made the post. She was charging that our fearless leader was a "racist."

Moreover, this board member also alleged that the superintendent was in cahoots with some other board members and told them how to vote. Further, she implored tax payers to come out and make their voices heard, as this woman was up for a five-year contract renewal with a salary of $1.5 mil.

Even though I felt detached from the situation, I was still amazed.

"All that money in a high poverty district," commented my inner voice.

"Epic dysfunction, good luck going back there," added the negative one.

All night long, I thought about it. By morning, I had hatched a plan. There was no harm in calling our local Delco newspaper and giving them an anonymous tip, right?

I called at 7:30 am. Naturally, I got an answering machine. I left a message and my number. By 8 am, my call was returned. The reporter sounded intrigued by the vague message I had left.

It seemed a good idea to warn him up front that I didn't want my name used. He assured me he had no qualms over that. I gave him the abbreviated version. He asked if I could text him some screenshots of the post, so I did. He told me to keep my eyes open, as this was a community issue that they would be covering.

After I hung up, I shot my buddy back a text telling her what I had done.

"I am perfectly capable of stirring the shit pot from afar," I told her with laughing emojis.

True to his word, the story ran the very next day. There were no regrets. Even though I had decided not to battle with them, it felt empowering to have thrown one last punch.

"You can exact change however you wish to," my inner monologue reminded me.

"How long do you think before you have another panic attack at work?" the negative one asked.

I really despised the fact that many times this gloom-ridden hag had a point. If I were honest, it was a worry. However, I was also a completely different person returning. I didn't care to bog myself down with all their debilitated drama. Plus, I was a true believer in karma. This would all come out in the wash eventually. That gave me a small modicum of comfort.

In the words of the Scottish novelist and poet Robert Louis Stevenson, "Sooner or later, everyone sits down to a banquet of consequences."

Chapter 14

February is traditionally a very dark and cold month, made even more so by the fact that it's the month my ma passed. Fortunately, this February was unseasonably warm. I was cold to my core as it was, and didn't want to deal with overcast, bitterly brutal weather.

An advocate from LTD had been in touch. He was to handle my transition returning to work. He had submitted all the necessary documentation and accommodations. We were simply waiting for Human Resources to approve it all. The district had a new HR head, and not the one I had all the issues with. I had made it known I was gunning for him, and like the true coward he is, he resigned. From what I have heard, the new guy isn't any better. So, we waited.

One day, Liz texted me to let me know McDickell had come to her room to let me know I was returning. When I asked what his reaction was, she responded that he seemed "Surprised." "Of course he is," my inner voice said, "more like clueless, honestly."

"Don't applaud yourself too quickly, McDickell still reigns," observed the negative one.

As despised as she was by me, she had a point. My principal had received no pushback for his lackadaisical leadership. This was not a fight I wanted to take on. There was no backing to be had in that arena, as I learned last year. My stomach started up when I thought about returning, but it was a done deal. I needed to go back, fly under the radar, and get back out in one piece. My sanity would be leaving with me this time around.

When Valentine's Day came a -calling, I went to the cemetery and brought flowers for my ma and pink carnations from my stepdad, per his request. I snapped a picture with my phone to send to him.

Hopefully, that would appease him. He was not on my radar presently, and I needed it to stay that way.

It took an emergency med to get me to her grave. When I stepped out of the car, I almost fell over. The cold winter wind ripped through my coat and froze my face, making my eyes water incessantly. My hair flew in the wild wind, pulling down my hood and whipping me in my face. Of course, it would go back to northern winter weather the day I choose to go to the cemetery.

As I paused to pull up my hood, a powerful Northeastern gale ripped the bouquet of flowers right out of my hand. I ran clumsily around the headstones, trying to catch them. When I finally did, I made my way back to Mom's grave and paid my respects. I did not linger and walked gingerly back to the car. It seemed a good idea to sit for a while before driving, so I did. I practiced breathing while I cried. This was one thing that would never improve for me.

Yet, I felt an obligation to go to the cemetery. My mom and I were the only two who typically did. I know my little brother and his wife went now also, and that made me feel better. I have cut back on how frequently I go, realizing it is another trigger for me.

Although a year had passed since her death, I still hadn't made my peace with it. I accepted it and knew I was powerless to change it, but there would never be any peace with it while blood still pumped through my veins. I often reflect on how many years my siblings and I have been cheated out of having parents. We lost our dad when we were young, and now my mom. She should have had another decade or so.

Added together, it was too much loss. I honestly don't know how people deal with it. A grateful attitude was what I was trying for on all fronts, but I struggled with it. I reminded myself that children lost their parents every day, and I was lucky to get the years I had.

It was a darn good thing that I went to her grave the week before, because I wasn't worth squat when the actual day of her anniversary came. In fact, I took emergency meds that didn't seem to help. The GI issues were back, and I spent a decent part of the day in the bathroom. I cried a lot and ended up going to bed early.

Thankfully, my brother treated everyone to take out. The next day, I woke up and cried for the first hour I was awake. Then I got back to the business of living. Or my current version of it, anyhow.

Three weeks later, we had an answer from the benefits specialist for my district. She let us know that the HR head had received the accommodation request and was being reviewed. I suppose this was progress.

As the days until my imminent return drew nigh, I became increasingly anxious. More days of consuming emergency meds followed. This was dismaying in more ways than one.

First, my overactive imagination was hard at work, devising all sorts of evil scenarios that always led me back to the beginning of this entire nightmare. The super had gotten her contract for 1.5, so nothing was bound to change there.

My inept principal was still in charge, and I use that term very loosely. The old HR head was gone, but the one who replaced him was said to be about the same. Plus, the vice principal, whom I had really respected and liked, had left.

Secondly, I had weaned myself off five meds since the summer. This was a point of pride for me. I was never one to take much medicine, and the GI issues were continuing to improve without all that poison circulating my system. Sure, they cropped up in times of high stress, but I was absolutely winning the battle with that, and had stopped losing weight.

Lastly, I had burned the Union Bridge as well. Once again, there were no regrets. Still, I fully realized this meant I was "unprotected" going back. Not that they had provided any last year.

All of this led to my decision to contact a lawyer. I knew I had a case, and could have sued them if I chose to. The ensuing circus that came with that avenue offered no peace. As much as I needed the money, I was not willing to take this route. Another firm belief of mine is that unnecessary litigation just drives up the prices on everything. My core beliefs were among the few things I retained as this changeling I had become came forth. I would not sway from my beliefs, but I needed representation to return. I would protect myself, because last year's tragedies were this year's strengths. I had done the hard work, put in the time and growth, and I was pretty confident that everything would be alright in the end.

Even so, I had to look out for number one. So, I set about this task, as I always did: with research. My chiropractor had been urging me to contact a lawyer throughout this entire ordeal. He assured me the one I chose was reputable. Two weeks after I completed the intake, I still hadn't been contacted to schedule an appointment. It's that weird pandemic syndrome, I suppose, wherein everyone works at a snail's pace.

Nonetheless, time was ticking. I reached out again and waited. Tom Petty had it right when he sang, "The waiting is the hardest part."

When I finally did hear back from him, the news wasn't good. Since good ol' Pennsatucky was a hire-and-fire-at-will state, there was nothing I could do but quit or eat it. I most certainly didn't want to eat it, but I still digested it. Why did I think there would even be an out other than the permanent one?

Possibly the most apt song in recent memory that my mind has played upon waking was Imagine Dragons *Wrecked*. This beauty played in my head every morning for a few weeks. One didn't need to be Freud to figure out that my inner soundtrack was mirroring my moods. Said moods flickered between anxious, sad, and competent. It was an improvement over depression, panic, and paranoia.

On a positive note, my sleep cycles were improving. I have never been a solid sleeper, and it was rare for me to wake only once or twice to use the bathroom. As a teen, I had a bad habit of sleepwalking. This happened a few times a month for years. It wasn't until after I was married and in my own home that it finally stopped.

To say it was alarming to wake up in a different spot than where I had fallen asleep was an understatement. When this would happen, I would wake confused, scared, and in a panic. There was no way of knowing what I had done while I slept walked. Years ago, I had watched a documentary wherein a person had killed someone and used a sleepwalking defense. I don't remember if it worked, but I am here to tell you it is quite likely possible.

Sometimes I would wake up soaked. If it had rained the night before, I wondered if I was out wandering the neighborhood in a nightgown. Or perhaps, I had turned on the shower and gotten in. Who knew? Everyone was asleep.

One time, my mom was working the night shift after my dad and she had separated. I was in charge of the house when she wasn't home. I had to take care of my two little brothers. I distinctly remember turning off the TV when the National Anthem came on. Yes, I am that old.

Anyhow, I locked up and went to bed. I put on my headphones and fell asleep to Pink Floyd's *Dark Side of the Moon*. I woke to hearing my mom yelling my name. She checked my room, and I wasn't there. She thought I had snuck out. I can remember being totally alarmed and bewildered. I was in my brother's top bunk.

There was no recollection whatsoever of removing my headphones, getting out of bed, opening my door, and walking down the hallway to my brother's room. I also don't recall climbing into the top bunk. Life is just weird sometimes.

Still, it was a dangerous and scary situation. I was beyond relieved when it stopped.

While searching for silver linings, I silently thanked whatever Higher Power it is that runs this shit show called Earth. The need to acknowledge, be grateful, and then move on was healing for me. This time, I was thankful that, even at my lowest point over the past year, I did not resort to sleepwalking.

Now that a full calendar year had passed, I decided it was time to take apart the photo boards from Mom's funeral. They had been sitting in a dusty corner of my living room, facing the wall, so that all that was visible was the white backing. We all chose to ignore them, even my grandson. In retrospect, that was odd because, as precocious as Kaleb may be, he never messed with them.

It was a miserable task, but I got through it without breaking down, and that was huge progress for me. I felt the first glimmer of hope in a while. The negative one had been unusually quiet as of late, but I won't question a good thing.

Life, much like me, was very slowly coming together. Angelica and her man had pushed the pause button on the constant turmoil. Her little family moved into a nicer apartment. This one had a pool, a gym, community gardens, and a playground. The best part was that she would no longer be across from the refinery. I drove to her original apartment many times over the years. The smoke and poison are pumped out daily. I didn't want my grandson in haling that crap.

Thankfully, he didn't drink the water, but he bathed in it. His clothes were washed in it, and his food cooked in it. No one can convince me that it is safe. My reason for saying this is that the same people who test your water tell you it's safe. Think of Flint, Michigan. How long have those people gone without clean water? The Woke want to out that clean water is a human right. Yet, no one really expressed much outrage over the conditions in Flint. Maybe at first, but the outrage died off way before the problem was fixed.

Why? Good question, and one I can't answer. I believe it is a lethal cocktail of poor government oversight, lackadaisical leadership, misplaced outrage, politics, poverty, and a biased media. Once again, I will bemoan why any of this is acceptable.

Would you drink the water in Flint? I wouldn't. As of this writing, the "boil warning" has been lifted, and I still wouldn't drink it. While we are at it, let's add in the recent (as of this writing) train derailment in Ohio. Chemicals are spilled everywhere, but the water is safe, according to the governor. The most pathetic part of it all is that people will believe it. I have a pet name for those who just blindly follow the masses and such: Sheeple. Perhaps you have heard that term before, perhaps not. It insinuates that people have become sheep. They just follow the herd mindlessly, not really questioning or thinking. So long as a phone is in their face, all is good.

That, in a nutshell, is what is sinking us. People are outraged, but not about the right things. They are buying into the division that is being sown. That's what sells —derision, negativity, crime, and outrageousness. Just turn on the news. It's enough to make a sane person insane. Not that I would know anything about that.

What I would like to see is a refinery, or chop shop, crop up in a rich neighborhood. We all know it will never happen. The same narrative — that the poor need saving—has propelled politics for decades. We don't need saving. What we need are Senators and Congressmen who do not pass Go and collect hundreds of thousands in salary, for very little work. Sorry, not sorry – I do not consider the unending investigations to be money well spent. It is simply another distraction. And a waste.

Further, our founding fathers never meant for there to be career politicians. One was to come off the farm for a term or two, then retreat back to private life. Again, I digress. Broken is another pattern I keep detecting on multiple levels. This is what I was attempting to break free from. It's all cyclical, Kindreds. And relative. Mark Twain had it right when he stated that "Politics is the only profession where you can lie, cheat, and steal, and still be respected."

Chapter 15

My days as a crazy lady of leisure were coming to an end. As much as I didn't want to go back to that routine, I knew it would be good for me. Apprehensive was my mood all day, every day now, though. It still trumped deranged. I had licked every bit of icing off my very own chaos cake and was paying dearly for it on many levels. I needed to snap back.

Preparation is always key, and I spent a lot of time reflecting on going back. Tina role -played with me and walked me through various scenarios. She always asked, "What would you do?" or, "What would you say?"

She did a pretty decent job of steering me away from the negative responses I wanted to give and had me be firm but not spiteful. This was good, because the more I thought about it, the more I was leaning away towards holding McDickell responsible. Yes, I know someone had to, but the way I looked at it, Karma would deal with him at the proper time. I didn't even care if I was there to witness it, and that is huge for me. I am a good person, but I abhor anything or anyone that acts unjustly.

It's not like it would be the first time I took some hits to right some wrongs. However, all the fight had gone from me. This was another monumental change for me. I could trust that he would get his. I did not need to facilitate it.

What I began to realize was that I no longer desired his downfall. I was beyond that kind of emotional immaturity now. It felt as if I were enlightened. I realized that confronting him would not bring me any peace, and that was my endgame now. As I have said previously, it was my self-care.

Although McDickell was dumb as a stump, I figured even he would be able to read my body language and notice my tone when I informed him of my multiple resignations. Our hardworking HR department didn't bother to get back to the vocational counselor from LTD. They sent one email acknowledging that my request had been received, and that's it.

If we were to rewind back a few months, I would be in a panic, pooping and puking. My overactive imagination would be working overtime to deliver demonical daydreams wherein I was always in an impossible classroom situation with no way out.

This had been my reality for years now, and it was hard to shake. I decided to minimize the damage and reach out to the new HR secretary. There were a few essential questions I needed answered in addition to the accommodations. Such as what would my pay look like? Did I have any PTO for ongoing doctor's appointments?

Unlike her boss, she answered promptly. We set up a call to iron out the details. There were no mental lapses while waiting or when speaking with her.

"Enormous progress," observed my inner voice.

"Just saving it all up for your debut at work," retorted the negative one.

I ignored them both. The news was positive – my pay would be fully restored, and I had three measly days to squeeze in four doctor's appointments monthly. This was no easy task, as they were booked months and months out. It's that post-pandemic phenomenon again. It seems they never caught up from years ago. Or they worked at a different pace. Perhaps more people required appointments, and the available staff and resources were unable to fill the need. I knew firsthand what that was like.

Whatever it was, I refused to be agitated about it. That went against my search for peace. If I couldn't change it, I rolled with it. For better or for worse, come what may.

As one day bled into the next, I was trying to tidy up loose ends. I did some serious house cleaning that should have happened last spring. There were still piles of leaves in our backyard. I had hoped they would blow away this past winter, but no such luck. My body still hurts, but nowhere near the excruciating pain I had tolerated in the recent past.

Still, I would mow over those leaves and call it a day. In fact, I wanted just to plant wildflowers and be done with mowing. We had ugly, patchy grass from the dogs, anyhow. Plus, we needed to lessen our workload. Neither Tony nor I had any desire to spend our two days off mowing and raking.

What I had been discovering about this new Jen was that she wasn't apt to spend much time making things look spick and span anymore. For someone who had always been a cleaning freak, this was a radical change. I kept my house uncluttered, dusted and swept- the rest of it just didn't seem to matter anymore. The dirt and dust would wait for me, unfortunately. Gradually, I began to shed the extreme expectations I had always held myself to. This was also self-care.

While I had perpetually been a big cooker like my mom, 30 years of nightly homemade meals had taken their toll. This was one hobby I doubted I would fully get back to. I was back to making a home -cooked dinner every night, but I was apprehensive about keeping it up once work resumed. Cooking and baking really just remind me so much of my mom; it is hard to engage. The days of crying over her daily were behind me, but some days it hurt more than others. Either way, the void was eternal. Losing Mom was an endless ache that endured. She was my puzzle piece that would forever remain missing. All I had were my memories, and there were too many wonderful ones to count. They kept me warm at night. This is another self-preservation tactic I have been trying to adopt: focus on the good times. Don't look back on the bad.

It won't change anything other than my mood, which is constantly fluid.

Finally, three days before I was scheduled to return, the vocational guy from LTD reached out to let me know my accommodations had been approved. I breathed a sigh of relief.

In addition, the new union president texted me for "the tea." He wanted to know if the rumors were true that I was returning this month.

"So much for flying under the radar," said the inner voice.

"Pfft, as if," countered the negative one. I could hear the eye roll in her voice.

Remaining as neutral as I could, I asked if Karen had told him anything about what had transpired last year. Of course, she hadn't. He wanted to meet up for coffee that weekend. I agreed.

"This should be interesting," mused my inner voice.

"He won't care, nobody cares," stated the negative one, very matter -of factly.

Again, she wasn't wrong. Indeed, my district did not care. They made that blatantly obvious last year. Although nothing had changed on their end, a whole hell of a lot had changed on mine.

For starters, I was no longer a willing participant in their circus. I can't go so far as to say I was impartial – I still felt they should be placed on an improvement plan - but our scores were so historically low, I figured it was only a matter of time before that happened.

Secondly, the detachment that I felt for a job I used to absolutely adore was no longer painful. This allowed me to be the outsider-looking-in. It was a role I was familiar with. Furthermore, it felt safe.

Moreover, I knew where to direct my energy now: my family and myself. Family had always come first for me, but there were times I missed softball, basketball and lacrosse games because I had to work. I am not saying that I will call out for everything, but I am definitely prioritizing, and work is pretty low on the list now.

Actually, it was odd for me to even be on my own list. I rarely worried about myself. In fact, I rarely thought about myself. I reflected on my actions and such, but this was not that. I now had to prioritize my own needs, or I would likely break again. There was no way I was going back to the abyss.

Lastly, I had let go of what I couldn't change and all the negativity that went along with it. I was achieving peace, and each day I felt a little stronger.

Unfortunately, I can't say the same for Tony. He seemed to be sinking lower, while I was rising from the ashes that had been my life for the past year. The situation at his employer was deteriorating, and he didn't want to start over. As our flawed human nature dictates, Tony was taking it out on those around him. He was constantly testy and aggressive. He had gotten into a verbal altercation with a police officer that week and was super on edge. I talked him down that night, and the next day he was right back at it.

When he came home from work that Friday night, I had just gotten home myself.

He was aggravated, as usual, and started his shit. I asked him, "Please give me a minute."

He wouldn't or couldn't. He stood directly to my left, a few inches away, barking out questions. As he did, he was leaning in closer and closer. My husband is a big guy, with a booming voice. I lost it.

"Enough!" I screamed, throwing my hands up. "I asked for a freaking minute, and you couldn't even give me that!" I was heated.

At least, Tony realized he had pushed too far, and turned on his heel and left. He reappeared about 10 minutes later with a bag packed. A weekend alone at the cabin is the best idea he's had in a long time. Tony very obviously needed some space and time to think.

There was no ill will on my end. I completely understood his despondence and frustration. Life was hard, parenting was harder, and if work isn't somewhat enjoyable, then the scales tip towards the darkness. I hoped he found some much-needed calm while away.

Meanwhile, I kept puttering away at cleaning. Between my back and my knees, I had to take breaks. This truly bothered me, as I was used to full steam ahead at all times. That is another change I had to make; my broken-down jalopy of a body forced me to complete everything piecemeal. Especially the type of serious, deep-down cleaning my home needed after my sabbatical in Hades. Tony was a distraction many times, and I hoped to accomplish some serious chores while he was gone.

"Body's not cooperating while I'm operating," I sang as I dusted, reminiscent of the lyrical genius that is Eminem.

Meanwhile, our little package of love, Kaleb, qualified for early intervention. At 28 months, he still wasn't talking really. I tried to help him, but my degree was not in speech therapy. He obviously understood what we said, and he did try to form words. He just needed a little help. I was especially grateful that Angelica didn't do what many parents do and stay in denial. Closing those little gaps early during a child's growth helps tremendously later. We all wanted our little prince to have every advantage he could.

Honestly, I have learned through my years behind the desk that exposure is key when children are young. Due to the pandemic, Kaleb had not interacted with peers daily. If we got him talking, and he went to daycare next year, he would be in good shape. I hope it's possible to speak intentions out loud, and that they come true when they're deserved.

As for the rest of the family, they had remained catastrophe-free for a while now.

Ella bought a nice SUV, and Aaron was holding down two jobs. We still hadn't heard back from the free legal aid guy who was supposed to call. That was a never-ending circle of dysfunction. Aaron was taking the meds, but some days his eyes were black. Other days, he was manic and talked nonstop. He came over weekly and usually spent the night. Quite a few times, he came and just slept for hours. I don't think he felt secure enough at home to get real rest. I was still vexed as to what to do for him. Some nights, I prayed to win the lottery so I could get him excellent health care. Yet, I had lowered my expectations so that, so long as he stayed out of jail and could pay his bills, I was satisfied.

All the anger and despair I had over Aaron's diagnosis were gone. That was some heavy baggage to set down finally. What I felt now was sorrow. Aaron had been dubbed the "golden child" by his sisters when they were all young. This was because he never did anything wrong. He excelled in school, played two sports, and had a small group of close friends he had been hanging out with since preschool. He kept most of those friends as he progressed through middle and high school. He ditched sports and took up music and skateboarding. I took him for music lessons weekly for years, and he excelled at both bass and guitar. Plus, he could read and write music.

In addition, Aaron was quiet, thoughtful, studious, and respectful. He could be funny, but had a very dry delivery that cracked his father and me up. Aaron was sensitive and shy, but was always invited to parties and sleepovers when he was young. Parents loved him because he was no -fuss, no muss. He had a BA in the Sciences and couldn't hold a job related to his major due to his illness. The ways in which schizophrenia changed him were atrocious. Some days, I barely recognized my own son.

My illness has changed me, too, but I like to think this shift is for the better. That remains to be seen, though. One major development was the new, all-encompassing acceptance I was feeling. I can't change Aaron's diagnosis, but I do accept it. This was life -altering for me because I could look at our relationship more objectively than ever before.

The same goes for my relationship with Tony. More and more, I was able to speak in an appropriate tone when he was getting hard to deal with. The old Jen would yell right back at him in the past. This new Jen wanted to know how I could help him get through whatever he was going through. If he wanted to be left alone, I left him alone. If he wanted to rant about work or the kids, I listened. But I would draw boundaries as I had to. Take, for instance, when he was antagonizing me just recently. I dealt with it respectfully and rationally until I no longer could do so. Then I drew that boundary. He was not going to take his anger out on me daily. I was understanding, but had limits. And that was okay.

My acceptance even went so far as to recognize that, whatever Tony had going on, the best thing I could do was support him when he wanted it and allow him the time to figure it out. That is why I let him fly solo to the cabin. He was going to implode like I did if he didn't get some time to put his head back on straight.

That entire weekend, I didn't text him. I gave him his time because I remembered all too well how crummy it feels when you are lost without any answers. He was working, which was tiring enough, but it takes a lot of energy to be mad all the time. Tony was probably sleeping the weekend away like a bear hibernating. I hoped he would return refreshed and ready to be an active partner in every way. Sometimes just hitting that reset button does a world of good.

Earlier in the month, we had talked about ways to improve ourselves moving forward. I had told him that he had to start letting go of some things, such as helicopter parenting our kids. It was a habit I broke, and it helped them and me. I feel that my relationships with my children are on pretty solid ground. His, not so much. His grumpiness and gruffness have worn thin on all three of our little adults. He had to start picking and choosing his battles. That is a hard lesson to learn, and old dogs struggle with new tricks.

I will never forget him asking me, "How do I do that?"

"Just don't ask," I responded.

"Don't ask what?" Tony said.

This back-and-forth made me think of the old skit, "Who's on 3rd?"My Cinematic Tourette's never let me down. I smiled at Tony and told him not to ask our kids about topics that were stressors.

"So I just don't say anything. Ask anything?" Tony said slowly, like he was tasting this new idea of severance that had never occurred to him. Truth be told, it hadn't occurred to me either, and that was part of why I had a mental breakdown.

"That's right," I told him. "Don't ask, don't tell."

Chapter 16

Spirituality was a new part of my peace process, too. I have spoken on this previously. It still blows my mind, though, how things start to fall into place when you actively seek peace, practice acceptance and gratitude, and welcome new beginnings.

Aforementioned, my deceased mother guided me spiritually when I was down and out. She also sends signs through electronics. Not only has she manipulated my car radio, I believe she sends uplifting and encouraging memes to me on social media. She knows I have a fondness for memes. These are not from her account or anything, but when I am trolling on platforms, feeling down, an encouraging meme that directly addresses what I am feeling or thinking will pop up on my feed. Most times, it is exactly what I need to hear.

My purpose is not to tout ghosts or tarot, or anything of the sort, although those topics are fascinating. I have done enough reading over my half-century on this earth to know that, in certain circles, it is widely believed that spirits can harness electricity and the like to make contact. As far back as the 1800s, humans have been captivated by the notion that spirits can manipulate energy. It makes sense when you think about it, since we are energy, and that is what will live on. Some form of it anyhow.

Honestly, I would much rather rely on this than risk attaching something negative by using Ouija or other means. Lights aren't flickering, there is no wind blowing, and no ghouls moaning. Contact with a lost loved one is much more subtle. You have to look for the signs and maintain the faith that they were put in your path for a reason. Also, having an open mind helps tremendously.

Over the years, I have had many paranormal experiences. Our Irish family is this way. My nan's sister read tarot. It is rumored she was part gypsy. Her name was Romaine, so it would make sense. Apparently, she was the result of an affair gone wrong. Her mother, my great-grandma, regularly visited a psychic. The story goes that the day before she died at the tender age of 42, she went to her psychic, but the woman wouldn't answer the door.

Instead, she stuck her head out of a top window and yelled down, "Just go away, for you have no future!"

Sure enough, she passed the next day. Odd, no? My mom and her sister, who passed before her, both saw spirits and possessed pre - cognition. The same goes for me and Angelica. Ella is the next level up; she was born with a veil. Spirits are majorly attracted to her, and they speak to her as well. They do not speak to Angelica or me, nor do I believe they spoke to my mom and aunt. Ella has chosen not to hone this gift. Or curse rather. She spent many years terrified of what she saw and heard before she understood. Alas, special talents such as these are much like muscles in that they atrophy when not used. I could write an entire other book about the things that have happened in this particular department. Another day, perhaps Kindreds.

Maybe you are reading this and agreeing. Maybe you are reading this and thinking, "Sheesh, this chick is crazy."

Either way, I am grateful you keep on reading, Kindreds.

Whether you think I am unbalanced or not, I am going to give you another reason to wonder: patterns. Suddenly, I was noticing decipherable patterns everywhere. That may sound vague and very odd, but it was true. It also sounds mad, and I fully acknowledge that.

However, I wasn't certifiably crazy anymore. I had built myself back up, carefully choosing which pieces were staying and which were getting kicked to the curb. I shed old habits, destructive behaviors and irrational thoughts. I replaced my more negative parts with acceptance and other restorative practices. Was I perfect? Hell, nah. Show me someone who is. Was I doing the hard work to "Build Back Better?" (Sorry, I couldn't resist.) Of course I was. I had scratched and clawed my way back from the pits of personal hell. I would return "nevermore." (I am a huge Poe fan.)

While I was a work in progress, there was no denying I had made huge strides. I was proud of myself. I would continue with self-care, mindful practices and drawing boundaries. It still felt uncomfortable to draw these boundaries. I hoped someday it would feel empowering, but for now, it was still a foreign concept for me. I was working on it. That's what counted. It helped me to be stronger when I looked back on where I had been. Mostly, I lived in the present and didn't dwell too much on my many months of madness. Here I go again, giving you a watermelon instead of a seed, but that's how I am programmed, Kindreds.

Anyhow, back to the patterns that sometimes-included numbers. Math is the devil to me, so the numerical patterns were very obvious, and for good reason. One day, I noticed lots of ones popping up: on my grocery store receipt, my alarm clock, the TV.

Shortly after, we were at the cabin. Tony, my brother and I were playing Yahtzee. It seemed every single roll for me had multiple sixes in it. I hit Yahtzee once with ones, and then with sixes. When we got in the car to return to Delco, Tony pointed out the odometer. It was all ones and eights.

Next, it was all about those eighths. My brother and I went food shopping. The odometer read 118,888. It was shocking to me. How had I never noticed all these patterns before? Or maybe they didn't exist then? I will never know which.

Each discovery of a pattern felt more urgent, like there was something I was on the verge of discovering. This was not my overactive imagination acting alone. There was also how people reacted to me now. Wherever I go, I notice people's eyes seem drawn to me. It was unsettling at first. The best reason I can come up with is that people can sense my aura. It's as if they could tell I had just survived a living nightmare. As I have gotten accustomed to it, I just give people a small smile. I used to smile big and often, but I am not sure if that piece survived.

Even though I have spoken on keeping the faith, I must admit it is difficult. I wondered if any of this was real or if I was imagining it. I waited for my inner voice to tell me it wasn't. She didn't. I thought for sure Negative Nelly would rear her ugly head, but nothing.

One thing that made me just like my mom was that I loved talking to complete strangers in the grocery store checkout line. I always sparked up a conversation with the cashier or bagger. In fact, I talked to people everywhere I went. Tony was the same way. It made for a lot of interesting times when we went to concerts together. I used to say to him, "We are teaching our kids not to talk to strangers, but we do it constantly."

One piece that I am thankful I held onto is my friendliness. You never know how your smile or kind words can impact someone. Someone who really needs a Kindred acknowledgement. Someone who may be teetering on the brink. A friendly smile or acknowledgement could be the only reason someone decides to hang on today. I have always been big on kindness, but it seems magnified somehow.

Until now, I had never had a reason to research number patterns. Google is my best friend for odd research. As I leafed through the results, I found that repeating numbers are known to spiritualists as "Angel Numbers." These numbers contain messages from spirit guides. These guides can also be called angels. Some posit they are our ancestors, long gone. Whatever you want to believe is fine by me, but the point is that the message varies depending on the repeating number.

According to USA Today, angel numbers "are often taken as signs for confirmation and directionality." To access this article, go to:

https://www.usatoday.com/story/life/2023/01/24/angel-number-888-meaning/107910800 02.

As I read, I learned that angel number 8 is associated with karma, power, and taking control of one's life. The eighths signify new beginnings. All of these rang true to me in my current situation.

Always curious, I dove down the rabbit hole known as the internet. As is the case when you are at the bottom of the rabbit hole, I couldn't remember which sites said what, but again, I am all about the patterns presently. What I was discovering was numerology, because it is part of the bigger picture.

Since I detest numbers, I was latching onto the buzzwords and explanations. The pattern I detected across all the sites I visited was that multiple eighths were a call. The Universe was telling you that you had done the hard work and came out the other side. Now it was your time to shine.

Moreover, I was learning that four eighths, like the ones I saw, meant an abundance of good luck was coming your way. Many sites said that our money woes will be over due to this windfall of positivity. It may sound stupid to place hope in such things, but it's no sillier than playing the lottery. There is no harm in hope. In fact, it is a necessary ingredient. Our hopes may change, but so long as we hold hope in something or someone, we are saved.

So, I hoped. I hoped for better days, a more solid footing in the world, financial relief, and, of course, health care for Aaron. I hoped Kaleb would start talking, and I hoped Angelica and baby daddy would keep working on growing their relationship. I hoped my transition back to work would go well and that I would land a new dream job. I hoped Tony got his groove back, and I hoped that death wouldn't touch us again for a long, long time.

How many of us have dreamed about hitting the lottery? Be honest. I know I have, when I read about the huge payouts that sometimes happen. Of course, nothing is as good as it seems, and the winner must pay exorbitant taxes on his windfall. Only a government of the people for the people would take advantage of a citizen's sudden good fortune, right? The public is told that it helps elderly Pennsylvanians, but does it? I have seen the county-run nursing home near me, and it isn't pretty. It looks like a giant concrete prison, with very few windows. I know I wouldn't want to die there.

Anyway, one night I was sleeping. I was back to taking sleeping pills, but that isn't my point. I dreamt that I was in a dark space with my mom. It was lightless, airless, and noiseless. Don't ask me how I could breathe in an airless space- it was a dream. I haven't dreamt in lord knows how long, but I was having a doozy for sure. I knew it was Ma because I recognized her jeans, blouse and sneakers. She was sporting a red-and-white plaid blouse with dark-wash jeans. What was immensely unsettling was that her face was completely blurred. I couldn't figure out why, and I never got a chance to ask her. She repeated to me several times, "836."

Then I woke up. It was pitch black in our room. I got up and groggily searched for a pen or pencil, anything to write that number down with. I didn't want to turn on the light with Tony out cold like that. I saw on my alarm clock that it was 3:33 am.

"Of course it is," I muttered to myself.

In the end, I settled for a tube of lip gloss that was on my dresser. I scrawled 836 in the corner of the mirror with the lip gloss and went back to bed. The next morning, Tony gently shook me awake and quietly said, "What the hell?" while gesturing at the mirror.

Sleepily, I recounted my dream to him. He stared at the mirror for a minute, then turned to me and said, "I will play that on my way home tonight."

"Good idea," I said, rolling over.

If you knew us personally, you would know instantly that Tony, in fact, did not stop on his way home. He did not play that particular number, or any number, that night. I asked about it when we went to bed. The red lip gloss in my mirror was hard to miss. He admitted he forgot, and I let it go.

This dream further cemented my belief in an afterlife, and it was the beginning of Tony realizing that, while his wife may be crazy, crazy things happen to her. He was coming around and waking up to the fact that I wasn't just a good story teller, I was haunted. I have seen things my entire life. Much like Ella, it was not a skill I chose to hone. Yet it remained.

Chapter 17

Lunch with the new union president went as well as could be expected. Mike was a nice guy. He had arrived in the district shortly after me, and we had gone through much of the induction process together. Mike's in-laws lived down the street from me. He had graduated from the same school as my children. We knew a lot of the same people.

As stated previously, Delco was just that way. Delaware County was like an ancient, giant oak tree with roots that ran everywhere underground. Most of us were Philly transplants, or our parents were. We constituted a large portion of Eagles country, and we lived for Red October. Philadelphians want to deny us until Nova wins.

So, we have created our own community that lives by some odd rules. I am told we have a distinctive accent, but actually it's everyone else who does—not us. I mean, Philadelphia is the cradle of liberty — it all started here. So in reality, we are the OG. Further, Delaware County natives are the only ones allowed to trash-talk Delco. We may have a love/hate relationship with where we are from, but no one is allowed to diss Delco.

It is an interesting way of life. I had been born in South Philly, but we moved out of the city when my dad fell asleep with a lit cigarette and burned our house down. My mom's parents, Nan and Pop, had just moved out of Southwest Philadelphia to Clifton Heights. We went and stayed with them because we were basically homeless. Mom was going to rebuild in Southwest, but a house came up for sale around the corner from Nan, and it was cheaper to purchase than to rebuild.

So, my parents bought it. I went from first through eighth grade at our local Catholic school. Lifelong friendships were built there. I still speak to the same girls I grew up with. My cousin Jocelyn, who was more like a sister than a cousin, went to school there too. Her parents moved out of Southwest and landed in Clifton a few years after us. It's funny how those roots drag you along.

We were made famous by the critically acclaimed HBO drama series, *Mare of Easttown.* However, a plethora of films have been made in our area. Delco was historic in its own right. Nothing compared to the city we bordered, but still worth a look. Clifton Heights, where I grew up, is the home of the Slinky. All my '80s kids will remember this toy. Odd nugget of history, but history nonetheless. Honestly, though, there are many historic taverns, parks and Brandywine Battlefield. I do love Delco, although it has outgrown me.

To get back to the seed of this watermelon, Mike and I had a pretty decent rapport. He wanted to know exactly what went down last year and what role Karen played in it. I detailed it all. He listened and empathized. I was brutally honest and told him my days of mentoring, MTSS, PBIS and Student Council were over. I informed him that McDickell was a horrible leader and that he should resign. He and the principal were friendly, but I didn't care. I was only stating the truth.

Mike digressed and asked how he could help. He talked about all the new staff we now have in the building. And building subs! Two substitute teachers. While this was all wonderful, teachers still aren't being given prep periods. Mike told me he agreed with the multiple resignations I would be giving. I stressed that I would no longer be working outside my contracted hours.

"Good. I tell teachers all the time not to do that." He said.

"Then what about teachers not getting prep? They still have to hand in planning, and can only do it at night or on the weekends." I replied.

Again, he digressed. We talked for a long time, and he was alright with me not joining the union. I filled him in on the failures and snarky comments I was handed as I climbed the PSEA ladder to Harrisburg. I suppose it was difficult to argue pro-union after hearing all that I had to say.

There was nothing in my epic saga that I left out. I talked about the letter I wrote to the board, with no acknowledgement of receipt, even. I told him about speaking to lawyers about placing our district on a state improvement plan. I illuminated him on the lack of responses from HR. He had no idea they were discussing yanking my teaching certification.

In the end, we parted ways as friends and colleagues. Mike said to come to him with whatever I need. It was nice to be heard and to set the record straight. Who knows what kind of rumors and speculation had been brewing over the past year?

Later that night, I reflected on our conversation. It was obvious I was still harboring some deep resentments towards McDickell. The rub was, I wasn't sure how to move past them. I thought I had, but being with someone from work just opened all those old wounds. I had two days to close them.

On Sunday night, Tony returned. He didn't say much and kind of avoided me. That was alright by me. I had no desire to argue with anyone. I stayed up late watching serial killer documentaries with my brother.

This was my guilty pleasure. Ella and I watched *Forensic Files, The First 48,* and *Cold Case* ever since she outgrew Disney. Angelica and I started with *Hocus Pocus*, then *moved on to Beetlejuice,* and graduated to full-on horror shortly after. When Aaron was a tween, a local channel used to play all the old *Halloween* and *Friday the 13th* flicks, but they removed the cursing and nudity. It was awesome. We would gather snacks and just chill in front of the TV with the lights out.

My dad had graced me with the love of all things horror. When we were young, he bought a VCR as soon as they came out. Ours was a Beta, though. It was supposedly better, but whatever. All we knew was we now had TV on demand, basically. We would walk to the local video tape rental place and get tons of movies.

Admittedly, it is difficult for those who haven't lived long enough, to actually understand what life was like back then. We had maybe five or six channels. Cable existed, but not in the form we have now. Dad subscribed to Prism and HBO for boxing. Back then, it was either sports or adult movies on there, and with one TV in the entire house, no one was getting away with watching R-rated movies. PG was a thing, but not PG-13. In fact, children's programming was still basically relegated to a Disney movie on Sunday night and cartoons on weekend mornings. Plus, there was always PBS, and occasionally an *After School Special,* which was always some dumb drama with a supposed "lesson."

Anyhow, Dad came home with this giant VCR and a copy of *Children of the Corn.* My siblings and I slept with the lights on for weeks. When I was really young, my father worked two jobs. Well, he always did —sometimes three —but he would come home at odd hours and wake me up to share a milkshake and watch late-night horror TV. These were the old cult classics, like the original Frankenstein, Dracula with Boris Karloff, and a host of others. Peter Cushing, Christopher Lee and Vincent Price became my favorite actors. They still are.

Back then, I was a Daddy's girl. My mom put the kibosh on the late nights when I was giving her a hard time getting up for school. Still, the seed had been planted. I graduated to *Tales from the Crypt, Elvira,* and basically anything horror. (Which of my local yocals recall the "Man Eater from Manayunk- Stella?!") My mom read horror, and had long since passed her love of reading to me. I remember wanting to read *Pet Cemetery* by the King of Horror, Stephen King. He was and is my all-time favorite, even though I don't agree with his politics. As a freshman in high school, my mom said the book was too sad and that she didn't think I was ready for it.

Of course, I didn't heed her warning and stole it from the big bookcase at the bottom of the stairs where she kept her library. I finished it in two days, so she wouldn't realize it was missing. I was the kid with the flashlight at night, reading after hours. Angelica had been that way, too.

That book was too much for me, but it didn't stop me. It fueled my desire for escapism and cemented horror as my favorite genre. This evolved to include psychological thrillers and mysteries. (Mom was a big Agatha Christie fan.)

Anyhow, when my brother headed to bed Sunday night, I decided to sleep on the couch. My knees were a torrent of pain at this point. I had undergone cortisone injections, but they didn't do much. I was scheduled for gel shots on Tuesday morning.

Plus, Tony and I have had the same bedroom set for our entire marriage. We needed a new one badly, but we weren't on solid financial ground and hadn't been since I went on LTD. The mattress had been replaced years ago, but it was lumpier than oatmeal. Neither of us felt rested when we woke up. My sleep patterns were off again, and I hoped it was just the bed.

By Monday morning, I was puking and pooping again.

"It's the pain," said my inner voice.

"It's your return to work," the negative one contradicted.

"It's a combo," I said out loud.

Monday evening arrived, and Tony came home from work. He didn't say much again, which is totally unlike him. I rolled with it. He would talk when he figured out what he wanted to say.

With one more day to go until the district owned me again, I turned my attention towards Aaron. He was without a car again, and had been for months. We went food shopping and did a few other errands, such as banking. He looked like he was finally turning the corner and getting back to himself. Or as close as he would ever get, considering he was schizophrenic.

Still, it felt good to look into his eyes and see him again. Aaron's eyes were no longer all black. I could see the brown and gold in his eyes. He always had pretty eyes with long lashes. I will never forget when Ella was born, the nurses fawned over Aaron and kept saying, "He is so handsome. Look at those eyelashes!" Aaron would beam. He was such a proud big brother.

Yet, he and Ella were still on the outs, and probably would remain so.

My Aaron had always been painfully shy. He had a tendency not to look people in the eye. The little bit of self-confidence he possessed waned as his illness took hold. Now, Aaron not only walked with his head down, but his shoulders were hunched up. It was like he was trying to hide from the world and sink down inside himself, becoming invisible. I could relate.

Maybe the medicine was finally working. It takes months of daily dosing before any benefits are reaped. I hoped this was the case. Either way, work was a day away, and I had managed to make sure another one of my tribe was tight. That helped solidify my resolve to get through the next three months unscathed.

The morning of my own personal "D day" was here. Even though I was super apprehensive, I didn't throw up. Still counting blessings, I gave thanks to whoever or whatever was listening. I went through the motions of my morning routine: Coffee in the safe, dark space of my dining room. While I sipped, I stared out of my bay windows, watching the trees sway furiously in the wind.

"March comes in like a Lion, goes out like a lamb," my inner voice said.

"Like a lamb to the slaughter," added the negative one.

That made my stomach lurch. I got up and dumped the rest of the coffee. This was another subtle change; I could no longer stomach coffee. I loved coffee —it was my lifeblood —but no more. It was time to fall back on tea. That was my first love, anyhow. It wasn't until children were born that I had to step up my caffeine game.

After showering, packing my lunch, and dressing, I put on minimal makeup and straightened my hair. With my hair down, I could hide behind it —that was how I saw it. The apple named Aaron didn't fall far from the mother tree, it seemed.

The traffic was light, oddly enough. I arrived there before I felt ready. I would never be ready, truth be told. I parked and headed in. Not many people in the parking lot, thankfully.

Naturally, I had forgotten my badge to get into the building, so I had to ring the bell. This drew unwanted attention. The attendance clerk buzzed me in with a look of shock on her face. I skulked into the main office to check my mailbox for my classroom key and any stray mail.

"Well, I never thought I would see you again," the attendance secretary said, settling into her chair.

"Well, I never thought I'd be back here," I offered with a weak smile.

We chatted for a few minutes, and then Doll, the maintenance lady, came in. She gave me a big hug, and I felt a drop of optimism.

Next, I went to the cafeteria. My lunch ladies had been asking for me all year. Liz would text me when they did, knowing full well I desperately needed that pick me up. They did not disappoint and stopped ringing up student breakfasts to hug me. A few students recognized me, and also gave me hugs, high fives and surprised smiles. I felt the optimism swell.

Throughout the day, a few staff members stopped by to say hello. Liz gave me a huge hug. So did my other ride or die, Josie. I set about the slow task of putting my classroom back together. The bulletin boards still had winter holiday decorations on them. I searched for my step ladder I had purchased for my room. It was nowhere to be found. Instead, I climbed on chairs and tables to take down the holiday décor and put up something neutral but welcoming.

After this, I moved bookcases around and was happy to discover I had not lost any books to the sewage that had been in my room last time I was in there. However, they had removed the radiators and installed split mini systems for Liz and me. Our classrooms were off the beaten path and couldn't be hooked into the main AC system they had recently installed.

There were no tiles on the floor where the radiators were pulled. I strategically placed the bookcases to cover the worst of this. I needed to sweep the floor where the bookcases had been. No broom or dust pan. They were gone, too.

Feeling a bit aggravated, I made my way to the utility closet to find a broom. I saw McDickell coming the other way and put my head down. It didn't work. He approached me and stuck his face in mine, complete with a big, shit eating grin.

"Hello there, welcome back," he boomed.

"Thanks," I muttered and kept moving.

Always undeterred, he followed me. I stopped at the cafe doors and turned to face him. He said something about being surprised that I came back.

"Yeah, because he thought he got rid of you for good," declared my inner voice.

I immediately piped up, so as to drown out anything that the negative nag could offer. "I am only back because I didn't find anything else."

He went on to do his "I am your best friend" routine, telling me about how he interviewed at our local school district years ago and the interviewers wanted him, but had already promised the job to another. Blah, blah, blah.

"Whelp, thank God because my kids went there and it's a good school." I fired one across the bow and waited for his response.

Fool that he is, he blinked a few times and went right on talking. I just saw the 2nd-grade team approaching. I worked closely with these ladies and pulled students out of their classes for intensive reading services. The first two breezed by me without so much as a mumbled "hello." The last one stopped and turned me. She offered a few words of encouragement, and I realized I must look like the crazy lady everyone thought I was.

At that point, I headed into the cafeteria to grab the broom. When I did, some 6th graders that I have had in the past recognized me. They screamed my name joyously and rushed me for hugs. This was so vastly different from the last time a student rushed me, I allowed myself to savor it. As I looked around, I saw that more than 50 students had formed a large circle around me, smiling and hugging, welcoming me back. That made the awkwardness of the conversation with my principal fade away. No one broke this up, and when I finally managed to pull away and direct students back to their seats, I saw the lunch ladies smiling approvingly.

When I finally returned to my classroom with the broom, I swept up the front and admired my handiwork. Liz came in and gushed about how nice it looked. All these little pick-me-ups, I held onto them for the days ahead.

It was time to conquer the back of my classroom, where my desk, supplies and Lending Library were. The rear of the classroom was a huge double doorway carved into the wall, and that back room held all of our state testing supplies. It also housed an electrical box and some computer stuff.

My desk and belongings were situated across from all of this. The Lending Library was stacked with books students had borrowed and returned after I was gone. They were good eggs, our students.

Upon opening the small filing cabinet next to my desk, I found that mice had been living in there. Not only living there, but defecating, urinating and destroying everything in there. Ten years' worth of masters, destroyed. All of my Christmas decorations, destroyed. My timers, hole punch, coffee pods, and other little necessities I had stored in the top were also destroyed. The situation was beyond gross, to say the least, and unsanitary. I set out to find Doll and see if she had a vacuum with attachments. Unfortunately, she did not. I would have to bring in my shop vac from home to clean up this mess.

Now, please tell me, Kindreds, in what other school district would this be acceptable? I haven't even told you about the mini split systems they installed. Tony does HVAC for a living, so I sent him pictures. He and his boss had a pretty good laugh at our expense. These units were so poorly installed that all the tubes and water reservoirs were hanging out of the system. Instead of tucking it into the ceiling tiles, they left it that way, with the tiles popped out everywhere. Tony informed me that the tubes were for drainage and cautioned that they would leak. By the time we needed air, state testing would be here. Let all the higher-ups see that mess, I thought to myself.

"You're kidding yourself if you think they will care," intoned the negative one.

"Ah, there she is," I thought. Yes, she was once again correct. Our admin would simply stick a bucket under it. I got through the first day and the next before things got super shady. Luckily for me, the first two days simply involved cleaning my room, setting up my supplies, locating resources, and, of course, cleaning up mouse shit. I tried to reconnect with as many staff and students as I could. Some were kind, others were not.

Friday was a half-day for students and professional development for teachers. I was given my new schedule by Liz, so I went around touching base with teachers and letting them know who I would be pulling for services, and who I would push into their class to support. Again, most were alright with me, but many more weren't. I took my losses as I took my small gains, with a whole lot of reflection.

People seemed to be under the impression that I was on vacation for a year and not having a nervous breakdown. I understood that there were teachers who would absolutely do this. But I wasn't one of them. It irked me that my incredibly strong work ethic didn't speak louder than rumors. The middle school teachers were having a Dip Day on Friday, and the one planning it all invited me. Everyone was bringing in some sort of dip for all of us to share and try. I decided to go and sign up for a dessert. Perhaps, they would be kinder than the elementary teachers were.

This was not the case. Only one person really even spoke to me — a fifth-grade teacher named Allie, with whom I had worked closely the year before my mental break.

When I stood to go, she said to me, "Do you feel uncomfortable?"

"Yes," I whispered.

"Don't go, stay with me," she offered.

"Thank you, Allie. I appreciate you so much. But I am going to go get a head start on our afternoon training." I replied in a hushed voice. I walked down the long, dark hallway to my classroom. I went in, shut the door, and had a good cry. Then I got about the business of completing my state testing training, which we underwent each year.

Since Liz was the School Assessment Coordinator (SAC), I didn't see her for the rest of the day, which was just as well. It would have been nice to make a few juvenile jokes about her being a sack, but it could wait. On the way home, I cried again. Why did people have to be so mean? And judgmental? For the life of me, I will never know. It's as Shakespeare said: "Hell is empty, and all the devils are here."

Chapter 18

Monday brought nothing different. There were still only a handful of people who would speak to me. There were no tears on the way home, though, and for that I was grateful.

My knees were a riot of pain. I had cortisone injections done the month before my return, and it did nothing. I scheduled the next level, which was a gel shot. Unfortunately, the next available appointment was the day before my return. I went, and it hurt, but no worse than my current pain level. The doctor informed me that these shots had to be given a week apart exactly, and the course was three injections.

Of course, timing is everything, and as it stood, I had to take two half days to complete the course of injections. This was less than ideal, considering I was just returning, but I was putting my health first. However, it felt like just another reason for colleagues to hate on me.

By the following week, I was at my wits' end. It was so difficult to walk the halls and be invisible to the majority of adults. When I went into classrooms to take reading groups, there weren't any friendly smiles, small talk or warm banter. I warranted barely a glance. It cut me, and I wished it hadn't. I wanted to have thicker skin. I was trying to, but my peers' childish behavior hurt me. These were educated professionals, and they were acting like the Mean Girls. When I could no longer avoid it, I went to McDickell. I needed direction on the grant money I had secured for our school the fall before I broke down. Specifically, I was uncomfortable going over his head, and needed him to find out how to access the funds. What started as a civil conversation quickly turned ugly. He wanted me just to drop the grant money and let it go.

"The lady who gave it to you is retired anyway," he grinned foolishly.

So, basically, let the district squander the money, because let's face it: they already had. Further, he made sure to say the grant money was given to me. Once again, Captain Clueless was setting me up for failure. This was no joke. PDE had awarded the grant. A government agency. My name was attached to it. I had tried to take the higher road, and it got me nowhere. I brought up what happened last year and let him know that I still felt very strongly about what had transpired.

He had the audacity to say, "Are you fucking kidding me?"

That's when I broke with all professionalism. We both devolved to screaming and cussing. I raised my voice first, but he dropped the f bomb first, so I suppose we were both wrong.

At some point, I got up and closed the door to drown out the worst of it. The attendance secretary looked at me when I did with wide eyes, and I responded by rolling mine at her. I turned back to him and told him exactly what I thought of him. I let him know he was a nice guy, but a horrible leader. I even used my favorite zinger: Your idea of educational leadership is walking around the building talking about sports and beer.

We went for a few rounds. He blamed everything on our former vice principal. What did I expect? He would never take accountability for anything. I told him that if he were a real leader, he would chip in more instead of just sitting in his office. He showed true shock at that. I am unsure whether he was shocked that I suggested he lower himself to help out, or whether he was delusional enough to assume he did.

At least I was able to tell him that he made me a pariah by acting as if I just went out on leave and milked it, instead of owning up to the condition of that classroom that finally broke me. His excuse was "I can't help how people treat you."

This made me even more incredulous and angry. "No one should have walked into that situation, let alone a struggling employee who just buried her mother! What did you do, stay in here? Why didn't you check on a difficult class that had a sub you had never seen before?" I was panting at this point and having trouble controlling myself. For once, he couldn't sway his way out of this, and he was combative because of it

There were a multitude of issues that needed addressing, such as our scores, but I ended up tearing up, and had to digress before I was escorted from the building. Both secretaries gave me dirty looks when I left. Or at least it seemed they did. Maybe it was my paranoia, which was raging supreme at this point.

Afterwards, I didn't feel any better. I filled Liz in with a bare bones story, because I still hadn't digested it all. She told me that one secretary approached her, informed her of the argument, and let her know it was "really bad." I couldn't disagree. It was. I was disappointed in myself for being so unprofessional and unhinged. However, I was more disappointed in the climate at the school. I never imagined it could get worse, but it did. Daily.

That night, I reflected on it and decided to apologize to both secretaries for my language and tone. The attendance secretary was very gracious and accepted my apology. The school secretary was anything but.

As I tried to explain how overwhelmed I was, she looked at me with what I took to be open hostility. I told her I was sorry for my tone and volume and language. She snapped back that "None of that has anything to do with me." She added that she was angry about the way I yelled last year when I had a panic attack at school on my last day there. I apologized again and told her I didn't exactly remember what had happened.

Still hostile, she informed me that she had experienced panic attacks before, and she remembered everything she said and did. This implied I was lying about my experiences with panic attacks. It was impossible to wrap my head around the fact that she was that narrow-minded. Her experience isn't mine, and I let her know. She shrugged her shoulders after I tried to explain myself further, as if to signify nothing I said would change her mind on me. I began to cry; I was so fried. Why do we all think that we, as a species, have the right to judge others mercilessly? Doesn't it say in the Bible that we shouldn't? Moreover, why couldn't she just have mercy on me and not be such a cold, dismissive, haughty bitch? Those who need the most grace rarely get any.

Luckily, a middle school teacher I knew came into the office and rescued me. We walked and talked our way out to our cars. I filled her in on everything. She was shocked. She had no idea that any of this had gone down. No one knew about the state of the classroom that day when I returned from burying my mom. Or about the fights. Or the student charging me. Nor did anyone have a clue they were covering themselves and trying to yank my cert. Now it was my turn to be shocked.

With all the gossip going down in that school, I found it hard to believe no one knew. Honestly, I think it was more like no one cared. Everyone was in their own personal hell just trying to survive. Although even this didn't explain the hostile work environment, I suddenly found myself in. I used to feel like part of a team, a community.

Now I felt like a leper on an island. The week drug on. Nothing improved. I could feel myself sinker lower and lower. I started taking a double med to combat it. I had not held on by my fingernails just to fall through the cracks now.

After one particularly dark day at work, I came home. The house was a mess, and my brother was lounging around, doing a whole lot of nothing. I sat down in my rocking chair and started crying. If it had to happen at all, I was thankful it was in the confines of my own home.

"This is better than in front of students," my inner voice reasoned.

"The students don't care, your bosses don't care, and your colleagues most certainly do not care. So why do you?" sneered the negative one.

As per usual, she had a point. Why did I care? Well, for starters, I cared because my students deserve someone who does. Further, I craved connections. I didn't want to be a part of a school wherein there was no community, just cliques.

Always wishing to inflict more pain, she followed up with:

"You are broken. They know it. Everyone knows it, except for you. Why keep trying? No one cares; you are alone."

Now I began to sob loudly. "Leave me alone," I gasped.

Do you think she would, or could? Of course not, Kindreds.

"Just end it, you know you want to," she said. "There is no use in trying. You're of no use. The world has moved on and left you behind. You don't matter anymore."

At this point, I was having trouble breathing and starting to hear that dreaded buzzing in my ears, my head, and my fillings.

"Just go!" I screamed. "Get out of here!" I meant "get out of my head," but I couldn't verbalize it.

My brother, who had been tiptoeing around me for weeks, was upstairs, and I could hear him shuffling around as I tried to calm myself. I didn't care if he heard me or the neighbors heard me. I was back in hell, and there was no escaping it as exhausted as I was, sleep eluded me most nights. Now I was sleep deprived, paranoid, depressed, anxious and in pain. The pain wasn't just in my back and knees now; my heart and soul hurt too.

Since I was already low functioning, the missed hours of rest took a toll. I still had Kaleb to take care of, so I talked to my psychiatrist and she prescribed Trazodone. It helped with my leg pain and anxiety, on top of knocking me out every night. I was very groggy upon waking, and hadn't dreamt in I don't know how long. That is why what I am going to tell you next is so bizarre.

Luckily, I had off this particular day off for a therapist appointment. I had slept like shit even with the sleeping pill. I was reading a book I had bought at the Franklin Institute when I chaperoned a class trip. It was about old ghost tales from places in Pennsylvania. The author was from Pennsylvania Dutch stock and had German roots as well. She did the most admirable job of gathering up the stories she had heard over the years. Her forward indicated this was an oral tradition, which to me is more accurate and valuable than anything the modern press puts out.

Anyhow, there was, of course, a short story by Edgar Allen Poe. The lens he wrote it through was Philadelphia, when his wife (and cousin!) was gravely ill. In this soliloquy, he details how the shadows have come again. Poe speaks of always seeing them on the fringes of his vision, yet he never can nail one down. He writes of times when he was very down and out, like when his step mother died. These were the times when you could see the shadows full on, not just dancing at the edges of your peripheral vision. Poe stated that he could hear them laugh.

Upon reading this, I had to put the book down. I have always related to the macabre, the colonial, and the Victorian. Past lives, perhaps my kindreds? I tend to think so now. We must carry little seeds from one incarnation to the next. Thus, my love of books, especially those by authors such as Poe, Hawthorne, and Lovecraft.

Just reading what Poe wrote, I was shocked. This had been my reality, too. I 've been seeing shadows in my home almost constantly lately. Two times in my life, the shadows had turned into demons that spoke my full name in a guttural, animalistic voice. It scared the dickens out of me, and early on made me wary of my sanity. Once, while student teaching at an upscale, private Catholic high school, I saw a flock of demons lift off the ground right in front of a bunch of freshmen. They soared towards me shrieking, and then disappeared. I recall looking around in a panic, as everyone else went about their usual routine. It was mind-blowing to me that no one else witnessed this in broad daylight. Yet, as Poe wrote:

"The boundaries which divide life from death are at best shadowy and vague. Who shall say where one ends, and the other begins?"

Listen, Kindreds, I know I sound insane. I probably am. But I also know what I saw and heard. I was not under the influence any of the times I witnessed paranormal activity. Nor was I on medication, or fresh off a mental breakdown. There are a multitude of experiences from childhood on. My mom giving me winning lottery numbers was just on a long list.

Chapter 19

The reference to the movie *Mean Girls* has already been made, but I truly felt transported back to high school. Once more, I was the one who didn't fit in anywhere easily. I was always the kid without a direct tribe. Back then, I flitted back and forth between Jocelyn and Kacey and their public-school friends, or with the rest of the grade school girls who went to our Catholic high school and flourished. I was not flourishing back then. I was surviving, each day the same as the next. School sucked, my home life sucked, and I felt alone. That's exactly how I feel now. The biggest difference is that it wasn't my dad who had just died, it was my mom.

Unfortunately, Tony and I took our angst out on each other. We were both stressed to the brink with work and bills. We were no longer financially solvent after my stay in hell. We were at each other all the time. It wasn't the first time we had discussed divorce, although I hope it will be the last. Perhaps not; life is just too rocky not to choke off the few beautiful things we cherish.

Between the nightmare work, watching the baby, and trying to keep up with laundry, cleaning, cooking, and dishes, on top of errands, I was beyond bone weary. This translated into losing the battle at home and at work. That further depressed me. The bills were becoming astronomical as well. Everything went up but our paychecks.

If I am honest, the burden of labor has always been an argument since I went back to college fifteen years ago. I was drawing a boundary that was over a decade in the making. My body was giving out on me, and I would be damned if I would sit in a house day in and day out while I was incapable of maintaining the majority of it. People kicking in with cleaning when they thought of it no longer cut it. I wanted out. Out of Delco, out of this house, out of my job.

"You could just get out of your life" the negative one whispered.

It was inviting. I had more and more wondered what would happen to those who depended on me if I were no longer here? Was hell real? Would I be reincarnated as a roach? As much as I longed for perpetual rest, I just couldn't get myself to "pull the trigger," so to speak. (Flaring irony intended.) There were far too many unknowns. Lately, I 've been caring less about those unknowns.

As expected, Tony was not happy with my proposal that we sell the money pit. He disliked change as much as I did. Plus, we had moved around enough when we were young and climbing the success ladder that we remembered how horrible moving actually is. I explained that we were hemorrhaging money on this house.

Finally, he agreed to speak with an agent about listing it. I wanted to find out exactly what we would have to fix to get a decent price. It felt magnificent to have a goal to get out from under the hardship of this house and the accompanying mortgage. Plus, our area was becoming far too crowded. Every ounce of open space was being developed into some sort of overpriced house or condo. This led to insane traffic and empty shelves at the stores. The supply couldn't keep up with the demand in my little corner of the world. I had no desire to go to three or four different stores just to complete my weekly shopping list. I had lived that life during the pandemic, and there was absolutely no way it would become "my new normal." Plus, I had no interest in going down for a road rage incident, and was likely to if we stayed where we were. The traffic was lousy, all day, every day.

That weekend, Tony and I went to the cabin alone. We spent most of it watching movies and snoozing. It felt good to kick back and let go. Work was heavy on my mind, and I continually pushed it away. I outright refused to let that place live rent-free in my mind. Still, I had the "Sunday Scaries" way worse than ever before. June could not come quickly enough. Monday bought much of the same. Thankfully, my schedule was insane enough to occupy me just about every second of the day. I was servicing more students than ever before since Liz was tied up with testing prep. It is necessary to note that one reading teacher was no longer taking any students because she was preparing for standardized testing. The other reading teacher was still a long-term sub. So that left me as the one and only reading interventionist for a school of over 500.

How is this acceptable? Especially considering that our scores had been released and LESS THAN 2% of our school district was proficient. Again, why aren't people up in arms? Instead, we give the useless cow running our district a pay raise and a contract extension. The teachers didn't seem phased. My guess was they were so detached from trauma after trauma at our school, because let's face it: being tasked with educating our youth and not being given anything feasible to do it with is trauma in itself for those passionate about teaching. Our students were becoming increasingly violent.

Administration was not providing much guidance on what to do. In fact, we were told to submit fewer referrals. I was still vexed as to why they had not been placed on an improvement plan by the state.

What's that student would be called to the vice principal's office, only to return later with candy. Naturally, those students doing the right thing witness this and lose their buy-in. The monumental dysfunction flowed. If this was their idea of "restorative justice," they desperately needed to open a book on the topic

As the weeks bled into a month, I was still the pariah. I had loved being a part of this community. I thrived on the banter in the hallway, the smiles and greetings. The students still loved me, and I tried to remind myself that they were the reason I had gotten into education in the first place.

Nonetheless, it hurt and I wished it didn't. I wasn't good at developing a thick skin at work. I was deeply wounded by the fact that not many "colleagues" seemed to think I was worth their time. Forget that I had done a ridiculous amount of crowdfunding on my own time to help keep our school store stocked. You know, so teachers could pass out school dollars en masse. Oh, and I also stocked their mailboxes with these dollars weekly for years.

Or let's wipe away the fact that I had spent so many unpaid hours getting PBIS up and running. Or the unpaid hours I spent learning whatever content they decided to throw me into, year after year. Who else had bought a mascot costume and hosted assemblies running around in it like a court jester? Again, my biggest issue was that none of this spoke louder than whatever rumors they had heard. Tony kept telling me, "Fuck them, babe. You are out of there soon."

Yet it incensed me that these public-school teachers —the same teachers who sermonize about anti-bullying and tout inclusivity —are anything but. In fact, they are bullies themselves. I openly winced whenever I saw one of them coming down the hall, sporting a "Kindness Matters" or "It's cool to be kind" T-shirt. It was hypocrisy at its best.

Lord knows I tried to hold my head up high, but it was hard. I cried almost every day on the way home from work. This made me miss my mom even more. She and I would talk on my way home many days, and I wished I could cry to her about how much I just wanted the ground to open up and swallow me whole. Mothers are the only people who will be all in when it comes to the treatment of their child, no matter their age. I craved commiserating with her. I missed her sense of humor. My heart hurts all the time anymore.

One of the unexpected problems with returning to work was that I had basically no immunity to the kids' germs since I had been a sheltering mental case for a year. I caught something in my second week back. It felt like the typical sinus infection that turned into bronchitis, which I was so apt to catch. Except this time, it didn't go away. I dragged myself to work most days. By the time the bell rang each day, I had no voice. My ears were full of fluid, and wearing my hearing aids hurt, as did every joint in my body.

Interestingly, I did not run a fever at all, even though every nurse and doctor who touched me remarked on how hot my skin felt. It was as if the scarlet letter of mental illness had burned itself into me. The shame and daily shunning had put me into a type of mental hell, wherein I burned eternally without a temperature. I accept that sounds far-fetched. However, I assure you this is exactly what I kept thinking, given my English major background. Hell, I had done my senior thesis on Nathaniel Hawthorne's son, Julian. It was titled "A Locust of Slander." Perhaps I should take a job writing for the tabloids!

After a week of this, I went to an Urgent Care. They gave me antibiotics and steroids. It didn't help. The following week was spring break, and I decided a visit to my family doctor was in order. Once again, I got the head honcho. He was cool as could be, but I still felt like he was afraid of me on some level. He declared a virus and told me to discontinue the antibiotics, keep taking the steroids, and he prescribed an inhaler. Further, he said if I wasn't better on Monday, go to the ER.

That Sunday was Easter. I had been going to cook, but canceled and went to the cabin. There was never any peace to be had at our Delco place, so I intended to go there and rest up. I slept all weekend, but basically felt no better. In fact, my cough had dried up and was sounding more like a bark. We drove home, and I went to the ER early Monday morning. They kept me most of the day. My veins were collapsing every time they attempted to get an IV in. They did chest scans, a breathing treatment, and a massive dose of steroids in the IV they finally managed to insert. When I disclosed my father's and mother's medical histories, they were concerned, to say the least. I was checked for clots, kidney function, heart function, full blood work up, et al. I was sent home with a referral for a pulmonologist.

When I went to see him, he did a breathing test and a full exam, plus we went over my hospital records. He noted that my white blood count was high and surmised it was something viral.

"Still, that doesn't explain you breathing at only 70%, especially considering you are on massive doses of steroids." His statement made me pause. My mom had breathing issues for years, and this scared me. However, I was completely unprepared for what he said next.

"We have found that over the years, teachers exposed to the same germs and illnesses- such as your bronchitis – end up with lasting effects This manifests as adult-onset asthma. "

Now, I was truly taken aback. Was work causing this?

"Any chance of going online for teaching?" he asked. I just stared at him. I needed time to process this new revelation.

In the end, he decided on a new inhaler with a spacer and a return visit in three weeks. I drove home, more depressed than ever, if that was even possible.

Chapter 20

As the weeks turned into months, I became less fazed by the toxic environment at work. I kept my head down and was friendly to those who were decent to me. Unfortunately, those people were few and far between. I still had Liz and was so thankful for her. Every year at testing time, she and I have to switch classrooms because mine has the double-locking closet for storing the tests. Liz works tirelessly in there preparing everything: pencils, highlighters, extra erasers, tissues, gloves and bandages in case someone gets cut. Snacks, water, testing signs, folders with scrap paper and scoring guidelines. These guidelines varied from grade to grade.

There are also accountability forms to be signed each time tests are picked up.

Plus: bathroom logs, Read Aloud logs, and envelopes for used scrap paper. This paper had to be shredded after the students used it. Most didn't. They were poorly prepared for this test, through no fault of their own, or ours. Administration directly bears the brunt of our unending failures across the board. However, I would be remiss if I did not state that the Department of Education is a joke in itself. It does nothing to tackle the issues in our schools truly. Instead, their solution is more documents and training. However, the training is left up to our district, and it is so poor it's laughable.

Sadly, that's the easy part. The true madness begins with assigning test booklets and accompanying numbers. These must be despiraled for small groups. The same test booklets can't be assigned to students sitting near each other to prevent cheating, but small groups require the same test booklet plus samples for teachers to do Read Aloud portions. Therefore, seating charts must be made for over 500 students.

The state has made a lot of money on PSSA testing, but not much headway with education itself.

Typically, the principal and vice principal take turns helping with this overwhelming process. Of course, Mr. McDickell was scarce. I chipped in where I could, and fortunately, we had building subs to help this year. Still, the testing itself was grueling, and the students were exhausted and cranky when it was over. About the only positive was that I was a small-group proctor and didn't have to see many people. My mantra became a countdown: six more weeks, five more weeks. I longed for summer and an end to the doldrums days. For now, I could only daydream about how freeing it will feel to drive away from this nightmare I call a job.

With Easter, Mother's Day and my birthday all occurring within one calendar month, I was feeling despondent. Everywhere I went, Mother's Day signs screamed at me. They were on TV, the radio, and the internet. How did people deal with this yearly, I wondered? It was not lost on me that so many others before me had experienced this pain. Why then, wasn't it getting better? Or was the majority of the population just that good at masking their feelings? Perhaps they were desensitized. My money was placed squarely on the latter, yet I still hoped it was the former. People are good at faking it until they aren't. I was a prime example.

So if we as a race are that messed up, why weren't more funds allocated for mental health? It is the elephant in the room and has been for decades.

My school was another example: one counselor for over 500-600 students. (Our numbers fluctuate because we have a migrant population.) How is that ratio even legal? I would venture to say that many mass shootings could be averted if those committing the crime were given help at some point. Instead, our elected officials will posture and grandstand, all while pushing their own agenda. Said agenda never includes throwing massive amounts of resources at the problem, which might possibly alleviate it. When will they get that this isn't a gun issue, it's a brain issue? Everyone is messed up in some capacity. I would lobby for therapy for all, but that's another topic entirely.

Typically, I am not a conspiracy theorist; I left that role to Tony. Yet one had to wonder whether this was a crowd-control technique. Keep us broken, downtrodden, and divided. We are easier to manipulate that way. This may sound far-fetched, but it felt true. When you are of a certain age and have lived through some pretty horrible shit, it's easier to believe that the people we entrust our well-being to are puppets of the worst kind. They sell out to the highest bidder. That is why Narcan is free, and EpiPens aren't. Big pharma is the boss with all the sauce. Many others are lining the political coffers, but the pharmaceutical industry is absolute demon spawn. My Nan used to call them "robber barons." She wasn't wrong.

All of these realizations just served to stoke my paranoia and depression. The latter was on the hard drive as of late. Honestly, both were vying for number one. It was difficult not to be paranoid when conversation regularly stopped as you entered a room. Alas, this was life. For now, I kept telling myself. When, in reality, it was bordering on two years of craptastic living, and I was well over it. The odd part was when I wasn't at work, I had emanated a sort of inner peace, and people were drawn to it. Now, I was hiding my light under a bushel, so to speak.

What truly constituted an epic burn was knowing that once things got better, they would soon get worse again, albeit in a different way. Was this middle-aged, I asked myself repeatedly? Does everyone in their fifties feel this way on a daily basis? Were our peers struggling as hard as Tony and I were? I found it hard to believe we were alone, although it felt that way. So why was no one talking about it?

Oh yeah, because mental health is taboo. Why haven't we shed that attitude in this day and age? We have the entire trans LBGTQ+ community that needs extra support. The Autism spectrum has been updated to include other disorders. It has become more specified, as it should. Yet, the resources have not risen in direct correlation to the diagnoses, nor have they even begun to encompass disorders classified by the DSM-5TR. Then, we have school districts like mine, where students are failing at every turn. The United States has more mass shootings than any other country. The money isn't going to the right places. We are supposedly the most powerful country in the world. How can this be so when we don't help our own?

The second epic burn is that everyone pretends to care about mental health, when in reality, those of us who are "diagnosed" with something, anything, are viewed as "less than." I was living this reality every day. Every time I watched a politician on the tube, I got riled up. They talked about everything, except what really mattered: the decaying state of our educational system, the mess our healthcare was, and the insane inflation that was slowly eking out the middle class.

"That's the plan," the negative one said matter-of-factly.

At this point, she had replaced my inner voice completely, but I didn't mind all that much anymore. This gal was tired of the pep talks, encouraging texts and memes, plus the hated self-care emails. If everyone else wanted to pretend our world wasn't imploding, I would let them. This did not mean I had to play the game, though, and that alone was liberating.

When faculty stayed for a long-winded union meeting, I sailed out of the building feeling light of heart. Never again would I listen to blowhards that lived to hear themselves spout shit. I was done with that life. I was noncompliant, finally. That lousy doctor was now right. This realization didn't sting as much as expected. It instead smelled like freedom

As state testing wrapped up, I became even more disconnected. I didn't plan as tediously as I used to. I no longer had to search for hours for usable resources. Instead, I found ways to use the bits and pieces I had without my teaching becoming totally dry, while still maintaining flow, being relatable, content-oriented, and standards-based. My younger groups worked with a deep focus on phonics. That should have happened in kindergarten, but they were virtual that year. It is a pandemic loss that our district had no plans to address.

Mainly, though, I put out fires and navigated fights, verbal confrontations and hurt feelings. This was the learning they needed. This represented the love they weren't getting. The fact that my hands were so tied just furthered my depression. I openly hated life anymore. I rarely had anything positive to say because I used it all up on my students. Mostly, I said nothing. Not at home, nor at work. I was content to half-listen and live in my head. That was my refuge. A dose of reality, a dose of dream – even when that dream many times amounted to Freddy Kruger.

Chapter 21

My most hated holiday has arrived: Mother's Day. I know it sounds awful for a mother to say that, but I owe myself the honesty. Luckily, all my kids worked weekends. Tony and I went to the cabin with the dogs. The weekend before, he had been badly burned and missed a week of work. He was out of days off now and had to take a few unpaid days. That was not conducive to making the mortgage. The negative occurrences seemed to never end.

Even though I felt like doo-doo, I pushed myself to do some spring cleaning. Afterwards, I lay down to read as a reward and fell asleep. I have never been a napper, but I was all about listening to my body now and not pushing myself to ridiculous limits. New Jen simply couldn't keep up. Although I don't think I am quite who I will be when whatever this is over. It feels sort of like a Limbo, or a state of suspension. I can't really explain it better than that. I knew I was waiting for something, but what?

Another teaching gig, of course, but it felt bigger than that. Yet, I couldn't quite put my finger on it. The negative one was not needed to know that, whatever the plan for me was, I hoped it would be revealed before I gave up. The edge was dangerously close again. There was absolutely no way I was going down that particular rabbit hole again. My fear was that I wouldn't ever come back this time. And being dead was better than that constant cauldron of paranoia, despondency, and isolation. The desire to check out before the monster of despair and madness took me back down again was strong. I was just waiting. In the wee hours of Mother's Day morning, I awoke to Ella's boyfriend calling. I didn't bother to answer and went back to sleep. Thankfully, I was able to sleep, as sleep was still elusive for me many nights.

When I woke at 7 am, I checked my phone and he was, as expected, on his bull shit again. He and Ella were breaking up. This was an almost weekly occurrence, so I wasn't pressed. I made myself a mug of half-caf coffee, hoping it would stay down. I called Ella and was shocked to hear her hysterically crying. She was saying all the things I was feeling: there was no joy in life anymore, she had nothing good happening, and felt so empty that she wondered if death was better than this constant pain.

Fortunately, Tony woke up and took the phone. He disappeared into the bathroom and calmed her down. I wasn't even good at that anymore. My anxiety was so high, I ended up yelling when I didn't mean to. I stumbled over to the trash can and threw up the little bit of coffee I had drunk. We got in the car and headed home. I did some crying after Tony fell asleep. I was just so broken anymore. What has happened to my iron resolve? Where has my ability to problem-solve gone? Why wasn't I getting better? All these thoughts swirled in my brain as I drove home. Ella needed a lot of TLC, and I was still good at that role. We formulated a plan for her to get a doctor's appointment pronto and a referral for mental health counseling. Ella was much like me and disliked the idea of daily meds, but I told her that is what it may take. She sadly shook her head. I knew how she felt. The last thing I wanted was to be stuck dependent on Big Pharma, but here I am.

Being the banner Mother's Day it was, I found out that Angelica had been assaulted again by her baby daddy. She apparently had to call the police because it got so bad. Of course, the baby witnessed it all Recently, I had been reading a book about childhood trauma affecting us in ways we have never known. It had started to dawn on me that this might be part of my problem. There was no way I wanted to see my grandson have similar outcomes. This weighed heavily on me, as I was not supposed to know, but honestly, what could I say anyhow? Angelica and I have always had a tough time of it, and I wasn't willing to go back to our old, volatile relationship. In addition, Aaron called and let me know he lost the promotion he was up for at work. Since his car was still out of commission, he was working locally. An early night seemed to be in order.

"Happy Fucking Mother's Day," the negative one and I said at the same time.

My alarm went off Monday morning, and I rolled over and slapped it until it stopped. Exhaling deeply, I stared at the ceiling fan over my bed, feeling a giant dose of trepidation. After a bit, I dragged myself to the shower. I allowed myself the luxury of a brief cry, and then got ready for work. Another product of the erosion of our school was that most people showed up late. I despised being late and came on time, until I realized virtually no one else did. I dreaded that place like no other, so in the end, I started arriving five minutes late. Then ten. Now I was about 14 minutes late each day. I knew I shouldn't be doing this, but if no one was going to say anything, then I was game.

Standardized testing was about complete, but that meant reading testing was under way for the students who are too young for the PSSA. I spent my morning doing that. A few made good growth, but more were flat-lined. It was another byproduct of the constant dysfunction within our district. By lunch, I felt the overwhelming need to cry. So, I went out to my car and did just that. There aren't words adequate to describe just how low I felt. I was fucked up, my kids were fucked up, and Tony was fucked up. My job sucked, my mom was dead, and my goal of leaving this district still in one piece was ebbing away. "Where does it end?" I sobbed. I knew I was suicidal again. Maybe I should sign myself into an inpatient facility like that bitchy doctor said? I mean, I was, after all, living up to her expectations for me.

As I sat crying, I wondered what it would feel like to drown. Maybe I could buckle myself into the Jeep and drive into the water? Mentally, I began formulating a list of local bodies of water. Which were deep enough? And was I really ready to do that? I am pretty certain suicide has cosmic consequences, and not the good kind.

In the end, Tony called me and talked me down somewhat. I thank my lucky stars every night before bed for him. He was the only one who 100% had my back now that Mom was gone.

That thought made me cry even harder. The only positive was that I had my classroom back now that standardized testing was done. It was comforting to be surrounded by my stuff. Truth be told, I would miss this space. It was nothing when I moved in, just a room with no windows and a chalkboard. There was an attached back room, much smaller, that housed PSSA materials and a lot of fiber optic stuff. I stay away from that part. My desk was to the left, and surrounded by shelves that housed my many supplies and books. It was a concrete cube with no windows, but I did make it inviting. My classroom was a student favorite. My! How I would miss the little buggers. Tears prickled my eyes again, but I choked them down.

"Bout time, all you do is wail anymore." The negative one intoned.

This made me smirk. I was beginning to get used to this crotchety old bitch. Her words mirrored my moods. More accurately put, my insecurities. The line between the two is very blurred presently.

Yet, as Pooh said, "No bother." Pooh was Angelica's favorite as a baby and early toddler. Lord, what I would give to go back. To have my kids little and cute, and somewhat manageable. To have my mom back. To be young and vital again. To not have my body betray me on a daily basis. To be energetic and motivated. To feel like I had a future again. Not to be depressed and anxious all the time. To not be dead inside, basically. Because that's how it felt.

The Tuesday after Mother's Day was a virtual Professional Development (PD) day for us. Depending on what you taught, there were various tasks to be completed. As it stood, I only had to complete Vector training. This is a two-hour training that the state requires every five years. I had just completed this about three years ago, but apparently the school district lost our records, so for those who hadn't done this in October (I was still on leave), it was the task for the day.

While I was annoyed again that our district was so inept, it did make for a pretty easy day, so no complaints from me. Supposedly, it was planned that way, and we were only required to work until 1:30. What a nice break! Upper administration rarely gifted us like this. My training was scheduled for 10:30-12:30. It was about mandated reporting and child abuse. The second training was suicide. These two topics were sure to lift my spirits, no?

Since I wanted to be proactive, I logged on at 10 am to make sure my credentials still worked. They did. I launched the introduction module and watched it. A short assessment was attached to each module. For whatever reason, I couldn't access the quiz. I went back and forth with several people from school. Nothing they suggested worked. So, I reached out to HR. They gave me Vector's phone number. I called. They made a tech ticket and said someone would call me back. I waited all day, and no one did.

There I sat tethered to my laptop for hours upon hours. I tried reboots, refreshing, and different browsers. I went to Vector's website and followed all the suggested troubleshooting steps. I rewatched the same modules, with the same outcome. Nothing worked. My last email contact with the HR secretary regarding this was at 3:37 pm. So much for an early day, I thought.

That night, I nursed the beginnings of a migraine from staring at a computer screen all day. How did people do that, I wondered? I looked around the house at all the chores I had hoped to do after the training. I just didn't have the stamina. This drove me a little further down. I was teetering on the edge, and knew it. Yet, there wasn't a thing I could do about it. I was taking the meds, seeing the therapist, drinking my water, getting plenty of rest, and meditating. Besides writing, what else could I do to make myself feel better?

In the end, I watched a movie with Tony and my brother. I figured it was "self-care." The next morning, though, I was deep down the rabbit hole. Tony and I had an argument that devolved into me crying uncontrollably. I got in the shower and had the dry heaves. There was nothing in my stomach, and I couldn't remember if I had eaten last night. I started having trouble breathing, and wham! There she was – the dreaded panic attack. It had been months and months since I had one. I had hoped they were in the rear view for good. It was hard to comprehend that I was missing another day of work, but what choice did I have? I reached out to my psychiatrist and waited. Always waiting.

The psychiatrist prescribed a double dose of the one anti-anxiety pill I take to get me through. The countdown was still on. I stopped keeping my head down in the hallway. Instead, I looked people directly in the eye, as if challenging them to say something —anything — to me. Many looked away or gave me a weak, unsure smile. It was probably childish of me, but it made me feel better to take more control over my emotions.

Finally, the last week of school arrived. I had packed up my classroom and taken a few boxes home each day, just so no one suspected my resignation. The only person I told was Liz. She understood. On the last student day, I penned my resignation. I gave it to Liz to look over before handing it in. I made sure to place it 60 days before the start of school so I wouldn't have to come back. Our district always holds teachers to 60 days due to staffing issues. Until now, that is. I received a long-winded email from the HR director, complete with every administrator imaginable copied on it. Basically, they were letting me go. Honestly, it is the first fiscally intelligent decision that they have made in years.

Now, they did not have to provide health insurance or a paycheck over the summer. Even though I had always opted to make less each pay, so as to have a paycheck all twelve months instead of the regular, larger ten-month payments. In the end, none of it mattered. I was angry, but also relieved. I decided not to stay for the last afternoon of recycled PD. What were they going to do about it?

As I wheeled my battered old teacher chair that my husband had gotten me out of the front doors, McDickell popped up. I ignored him and kept moving. Tony had gotten me the chair when I started over eight years ago, because they gave me a low wooden desk chair that didn't even reach my desk. That sad, scarred wood chair looked like a relic from the 60 s when the building was built. I had no doubt it was. Forcing my chair into the Jeep, I climbed in and turned up the satellite radio to a heavy-metal station. I wanted to peel out of the parking lot, but I kept my cool. I drove away, banging my head to Slipknot, and didn't look back.

When Tony got home that night, I let him know that the district had given me one last "for you." He took it in stride. I would have to get on his benefits and find a tutoring gig to get us through. Not to mention, pepper the web with resumes and form job hunts. That in itself felt like a full-time job, in addition to babysitting Kaleb. There never seemed to be enough hours in the day anymore - even with it being light out until 9 pm!

My brother, who had been struggling so badly, was still with us. He had graduated from his school program, but was languishing. Originally, the deal was that he would stay with us until he could get the help he needed and then move into an apartment. He was an Army veteran, so he relied on the VA for treatment. Since they were another inept government agency, they always screwed up his appointments and medications. He couldn't just eat it and get it all straightened out like an adult should. Instead, he would scream at them on the phone. Sometimes they hung up first, other times he did. If he waited too long in the Philly facility for an appointment, he would get up and leave. Sometimes he fought with the staff on his way out, or while waiting. This was why he wasn't always on the meds he should be on.

In his defense, the VA is severely understaffed and poorly run. It is most certainly worth noting that these facilities, hospitals, and programs are designed to help those who have done the time for Uncle Sam. Many are men and women who have sacrificed enormously. Why then is this allowable? Why are veterans repaid with sub par services and crummy health care? The pattern perpetrates, and the government just keeps doing what it does best anymore: subvert, avoid, and deflect. Needless to say, the mental health services which so many vets are in dire need of are undermanned, overtaxed and downright shoddy. My father was another perfect example of this broken system. He did time in 'Nam with the Marines. He drank himself to death at the tender age of 45. Furthermore, Dad never spoke of it. He internalized all the horrors he saw and lived through. His preferred coping mechanisms were beer and cigarettes. A lot of both. All the time.

My brother reminded me so much of my father, and it wasn't just because he looked exactly like him. He hadn't served during battle time, yet failed to thrive in the military. Couple that with the childhood abuse, and voila! You end up with the powder keg that was my broski. His life seemed to follow this broken trajectory. The worst part of it all was that he could not seem to change it. Nor did he appear to care to.

It is the same deal with his bank. He was forever cussing and fussing at them on his cell. It really amped up my already heightened anxiety. I had taken to staying away from him because he was always angry. He said some unkind things about my kids and grandson to me, too. I chose the higher road because I knew he was struggling. Hell, we all still are.

Naturally, no one wants to deal with the irrational, angry guy, so I suspect he was once again without meds. Asking him wasn't worth the shit storm it was likely to cause. His psychiatrist had strongly advised therapy too, but that was just another facet of his dysfunction - he rarely followed through with any of those appointments. Further, the VA promised him housing months ago. Yet, it never seemed to materialize. He lost his job when he got into a fight with his boss. This isn't the first time that has happened, and sadly, it won't be the last. He was just a hot mess that couldn't or wouldn't get it together.

Meanwhile, tutoring was a dry business this particular summer. I will fully admit I didn't put a ton of effort into it. To me, finding a teaching job for the fall was much more important. Those applications take hours to complete. A resume, cover letter, clearances, certifications, degrees, references and an essay. That was in addition to the multitude of questions to answer. Always striving for gratitude, I thanked whoever ran this circus for at least allowing me the brain power to complete these in-depth tasks. It felt like forever, but it had only been a mere year ago when I was crying my way through disability and insurance paperwork. I feel so much stronger now.

A few weeks before vacation, I got an email inviting me to a Zoom interview (what we in the biz call a "screener") for a local, upscale public school. I was thrilled. Most of my time at the cabin that weekend was spent preparing for the interview. I researched the school, demographics, graduation rates and national scores. I scoured articles for tips on teacher interviews.

On Saturday afternoon, Angelica called. She had mandatory training at work on Tuesday, the same time as my interview. I assured her that I would ask Jocelyn's daughter, Sara, to watch Kaleb while I was on Zoom. We chatted for a few minutes and hung up. I was stalling, making the drive into town for supplies. Tony knew why, and this must have jogged his memory.

"Did we ever check to see if your number came out?" he asked, opening the app on his phone.

Not my number, I thought absently, my mother's number. Tony was referring to the number 836 that my mom kept repeating to me in my one and only dream about her. This was months ago, but he seemed to remember it just now. I knew he would ask me next for the date, so I opened up my phone to the screenshot I had taken of the lip gloss number before we had carried it outside for big trash day. Thankfully, we had gotten a new set for our room. The time stamp showed the exact date and time. He looked at it and then opened the lottery app, scrolled down a bit, and his eyes got huge.

He looked at me, then back at the phone, as if to make sure he checked the right date. Satisfied that he did, he turned to me. "836, right?" he asked.

I nodded. "It came out," he said in an incredulous tone. "That same night. It came out straight. 836. See?" he asked, turning his phone towards me.

Not one to look for proof anymore, I just shrugged. Faith is believing without any proof, and I did. I knew that number would come out that night. I didn't need to check. Since Tony appeared to be having a hard time wrapping his mind around this, I decided it was time to quit stalling and get on with my errands.

"Do not forget to call Sara, Jen," Tony said over his shoulder as I opened the front door.

I gave him a thumbs-up on my way out the door.

"Call Sara" I reminded myself as the engine turned over. The Fleetwood Mac song of the same name came on. These synchronicities were amazing to me. While I listened to Stevie sing, I thought, "Ok, Mom, what you got for me today?" Remember, Kindreds, I am convinced she uses my radio to communicate. She can also manipulate electricity and technology. Some will believe this, some will not. It's okay either way. Have I mentioned Fleetwood was her favorite band?

Possibly the worst part about the drive into town was the fact that I had to go by my mom's old place. Typically, I cried. Listening to the old Fleetwood tune, my eyes filled up. I began to weep in earnest. Between sobs, I said, "Goddamn it! I miss you so much, Mom! Life just isn't fun anymore, and you left a hole so big I can't fill it." I dissolved into sobs as her place loomed large on my right.

Just as I passed by her development, the next song came on. It was the Eagles singing *Wasted Time*. The Eagles were an old favorite of both Mom and me. Suddenly, I could feel her presence right there with me in the Jeep. Continuing to cry, I said, "I understand what you are trying to tell me, Mom. I am mourning you and the time we didn't have together. Meanwhile, I am wasting the time I have been given on grief. Although I would never consider time spent thinking of you as wasted."

Suddenly, the sobs stopped, and the tears began to dry. I took in deep watery breaths. A panic attack on these twisty mountain roads could be deadly, and most certainly was not on my list of things to do that day. Trust me, it isn't lost on me that a short time ago, I wanted to die, but didn't have the guts to do it. Now, here I was wanting to live. To carry on. To figure out what was next. The last song to come on was *Moonshadow* by Cat Stevens. I had heard this song a million times before, but I had never really heard it. I listened intently to the lyrics as I zoomed down the mountain towards town. I had the radio blaring, the sun was shining, and wild flowers dotted the landscape.

What I was realizing was that Mom was with me. She wasn't that sappy "in my heart" stuff, although that was true too. She was actually with me in the right here and the right now, because our energy lives on. Our spirits, souls, whatever terminology you would like to use. I marveled for a moment, but then chuckled to myself. She was the most headstrong woman I knew, and coming from me, that was a lot.

"Of course you come back. Who could stop you?" I laughed. "You were stubborn as a mule in life, and you remain so in the after life."

My hair blew in the warm, clear mountain air as my Jeep sailed down the mountain. I felt good for the first time in a very, very long time.

"And if I ever lose my legs,
I won't moan and I won't beg,
Oh, if I ever lose my legs, oh if,
I won't have to walk no more

Chapter 22

We took our yearly family vacation at the cabin. Angelica and the baby came from Monday to Friday. We had such a good time with Kaleb at the pool, the playground, and the carnival. We took him out to breakfast at an old mountain diner that had cars zooming by the big windows. Kaleb loved watching cars. He was in his element, and it showed. He brought so much joy to our lives regularly. Tony and I had taken to privately calling him "our little Prozac."

Ella and Aaron were coming from Friday to Sunday. They would go home with us. Both of their cars were on the fritz again. Once more, I was head chauffeur, and it sucked righteously. They had an uneasy truce going at the moment. Ella, much like her mother, was an empath at heart. In fact, she had a heart so big it often ended up broken. Aaron, also like me, was just hanging onto whatever life raft he could find at the moment.

My mom's surviving sibling gave them a lift. She has a place not far from me, as I have mentioned before. Aaron was pale, waxy and moaning in the back seat when they arrived. He had alcohol poisoning. My aunt raised her eyebrows at me, but said nothing, thankfully.

Unbelievably, he tried to drink alcohol about an hour later. He promptly threw up and spent the rest of his first day doing just that. Tony and I gazed at each other over the campfire we were enjoying. I knew he was thinking, "What the hell do we do with this kid?"

I knew, because I was thinking the same exact thing.

Vacation ended, and I went crashing back to reality (I am an Eminem fan for those who read that in his voice). We drove home late Sunday night, mostly in silence. No one wanted to go back to the Delco house. Or the grind. Or my brother.

Who did nothing while we were gone, but soaked up the AC and ran up my electric bill watching Sports Center round the clock. He didn't look for a job; he didn't find out anything about this supposed housing. He just lay on the couch.

"Must be nice," I thought. This was followed on the heels of another: "Maybe he could have gotten off his ass and mowed our lawn!"

For months now, I had been tip toeing around him because he was a ticking time bomb. He continued to be unapproachable and nasty. When we came home, he moved himself up to the bedroom he was staying in, and didn't leave. A few days later, he came out and showered. He must have been having a semi-good day, because after showering, he transplanted to the couch to lie watching - you guessed it, Kindreds - Sports Center.

As I carried laundry up and down the steps, I gazed over the bannister at him, wondering what the hell went on in his head. How could he be okay with just mooching off his sister, who wasn't even working? How could he be alright with knowing Tony was busting his butt on a hot roof all day while he lay around sucking up what little resources we had? Most importantly, how can he sit here listening to Tony mowing our large lawn in 90-degree heat after working in it all day?

"Like you are a grown ass man, fix yourself," I mumbled as I dragged another basket of laundry up the steep steps. "Don't get up and help or anything," I thought bitterly. A storm was brewing, and I desperately wanted to avoid it. My brother had been dealt a hard hand as a kid. Yet, his actions as an adult did him no favors. Jack London famously said, "Life is not always a matter of holding good cards, but sometimes, playing a poor hand well."

"You can't save everyone, Jen," my inner voice whispered.

It was then that I realized I had not heard from Pessimistic Patty since leaving my job. Now there was a tiny, bright spot on my horizon. If I can just grow it a little larger, maybe there will be full-on sunshine in my life again?

Chapter 23

When my brother next emerged from his room, I asked him again about the apartment he was waiting for. "Can't they provide emergency housing since it has taken this long with no end in sight?" I asked.

He looked at me, and I saw that his eyes were beginning to resemble Aaron's when he was deep down the abyss. He promised to find out. There was no way I was going through what Aaron put us through with his mental breaks. I just couldn't do it. I loved my brother and wanted him to get better. The problem was that he didn't seem to want to get better. He was content to couch surf at my house for eternity. I knew that if he stayed much longer, our relationship would most likely become irreparable. I was trying supremely hard not to let that happen. He was my family, I loved him dearly, and I lost too many to let it slide.

Although I felt like an enabler, if I continued to let him be a bum, he would be, in the way I see it. Broski was in a broken pattern. He has lived with us on and off throughout our entire marriage. I was tired of cleaning up after him. He thought he cleaned up, but it was always a half ass job. He refused to rinse his dishes before putting them in the dishwasher. As a result, our two -year-old dishwasher smelled like a compost heap on a hot day. The free room we provided him with was a pig sty - stuff all over the floor, counters, and dresser. Moreover, he had pulled out important things I had stored in the large closet and thrown them into a corner. He had knocked down clothes and left them there. It was infuriating.

One morning after dropping Ella at work, I went food shopping. I wrote a check, hoping it wouldn't be posted until Tony's payroll did. This is what we had come to. Our years of doing that dance were far past us, or so we had thought. It was humbling to realize we were full circle in the finance department.

When I got home, I cleaned the fridge of old food, not that there was much. When I did, I realized there was chocolate milk spilled all down the fridge, and it was syrup by the time I found it. I couldn't get it off. The fridge had been replaced recently, too, and I was boiling over at this discovery. I snapped a pic with my phone, and sent the same exact picture and caption to the three adults I live with. Tony offered to clean it up. Ella apologized. My brother sent a bunch of snarky messages back, telling me to "get out of here with that shit." Get out of here? This was my house. I knew he was using a figure of speech, but he broke my reserve. I sent back a long-winded reply, filling him in on how ungrateful he was. He ignored me. I waited for a few hours. Kaleb got dropped off, and Ella came home from work. Me? I simmered.

Finally, I went upstairs and didn't bother to knock. I let him have it. I told him I wanted him gone. Originally, I was willing to wait to let him sort it out, but I wanted a concrete date of when he was moving. He decided that just like everyone else he dealt with, he would react to this inconvenience (that he created) by being a rude, vile, prick back to me. We went at it, and I asked for my keys back. He threw them at me. Hard.

At this point, Kaleb woke up crying, and I went downstairs to get him. Bro followed me, yelling, but stopped at the top of the stairs. I descended the stairs, screaming back. This was over a year's worth of putting up with his bull shit on top of everything else. As I said, he broke down my resolve with his negative ass attitude on top of using avoidance as his only tool.

When my brother bounded down the steps a few minutes later, he had a suitcase and a bag. He looked wild and unhinged. I was rocking Kaleb in my pink chair, and I felt my mouth go dry. He came within five feet of me and screamed at the top of his lungs. Granted, I had been screaming at him too upstairs, but what he said in front of my grandson - his great nephew - is incorrigible and unprintable.

Ella was now in the living room, and I handed Kaleb off to her as I followed my brother to the door. He was known for breaking things when he was angry, and I wasn't about to let him bust a window on his way out. At this point, he turned around and screamed at me that, "I needed help!" Funny, cause I take my meds and do the therapy, unlike him. I realize, though, that most people don't own or even recognize their shit: traumas, issues, negative behaviors and so on. My brother was no different.

It was at this point that I launched my final weapon:

"And you are nothing but a freeloader!"

He turned to me as he was walking out the door. His eyes were as black as coal. It occurred to me again that he looked much like Aaron did in a crisis. I guess I hit a nerve when I spat his truth, because he turned in the doorway with a closed fist, ready to connect it with my face. I pushed the door with all my weight, and it closed on him. I quickly locked it. He stood screaming and giving me the finger with one hand, while shaking a closed fist at me with the other. He then proceeded down my driveway bellowing "Fuck you!" as he went. I am sure my neighbors loved that. He was supremely lucky Tony was not around when this went down, because he would have kicked my brother's ass -not only for speaking to me that way in our own home, but also in front of Kaleb. The punch he tried to throw would just be the final nail in his casket.

While I felt terrible that this went down the way it did, I was incredibly relieved that it was just Tony, Ella and me again. In the days that followed, I flitted back and forth from indignant and righteous to sad and depressed. I knew Mom would be sorely disappointed in both of us for the way we acted when it got super heated. However, I also knew I was drawing an essential boundary with him. No longer would I feel like a stranger in my own home. I just wish he could have handled the entire situation better, because once he launched into attack mode, my flimsy reserve crumbled. I fired right back with some very ugly truths about him that he didn't like. Perhaps some of my Kindreds are thinking, "Stay in your lane, lady."

My issue is he was in my lane, and my kitchen, and my bathroom! You get my point, I am sure, but the fact that he had entirely stopped cleaning up or contributing was beyond my comprehension. Yes, I had done the same at one point, but I was in my own home, with my husband of over 30 years. I had grown children who took turns needing me. Plus Kaleb. I could not raise my brother. He had lived with us for over 9 years altogether. That is almost a third of our marriage! He was incredibly blessed that Tony viewed him as his own little brother, or else he would not have dealt with him for that long either. The entire year of frustration with his lack of accountability and initiative took its toll. Once I removed the lock from that particular Pandora's Box, it was a done deal. I could no longer keep my mouth shut. All restraint, shattered. Moreover, one does not come back from the crazy he had going on without some serious self-reflection and hard work. I personally knew this to be true.

Still, I missed him, worried about him, and loved him. I fully realized I only had one brother left now - my youngest bro, who was twelve years my junior. I had always been tighter with the other one because he was closer in age to me.

Aforementioned, my brother spent a lot of time with us. My children and nieces (Jocelyn's girls) had dubbed him long ago, "Uncle Amusement Park." This was another way he reminded me of Dad; our father was fantastic with kids. The tradition had continued on with Kaleb. In his early days of living here, he would play with Kaleb all the time. I loved listening to Kaleb's squeals of joy as my brother tickled and wrestled him. I knew it brought them both happiness and contentment, too. Brohemian would change diapers, cook, and do dishes. Over time, he just didn't bother anymore. I missed his help. Our laughs. Damnit, I missed my brother.

Our rift had a negative effect on me. I was back to puking, not eating and not sleeping. There were dark circles under my eyes, and I had started losing weight again. Oddly enough, I did not cry.

Furthermore, he had blocked all of us on social media, so there was no way to know if he was safe, dead, or in jail. If the latter proved true, I wouldn't be shocked because it would by no means be his first rodeo in county lockup. Luckily, my sister-in-law was able to track his phone. She found out he was at a VA hospital in another county seeking services, hopefully, for intense mental help.

"Why couldn't he just carry through with that back when he was supposed to?" my mind screamed. Perhaps then, none of this would have transpired.

Chapter 24

Summer was sweeping by, in that lazy way it did, that caught you off guard when August arrived. My job hunt continued, but my phone never rang. Discouraged, I remember Tony warning me: "I hope what happened doesn't spread around to other Delco schools."

At the time, I can remember thinking, "That wouldn't happen. That couldn't happen." Now, I wondered in earnest. How closely related were the schools in my area? How quickly did word travel? Was I branded as broken or poison perhaps? I also remember the negative one telling me not too long ago that I was "broken, and everyone can see it." This pushed me down a little further, and I allowed myself to wallow in it for a bit.

It hurt that, with all my credentials and experience, I wasn't getting interview offers, let alone teaching positions! The law dictates that employers can't say anything outwardly negative about a person when they leave a job. But let's be real here for a second. It happens. Perhaps my district continued to screw me at will. Perhaps I was just paranoid.

Honestly, the Department of Ed had finally decided to address the teacher shortage. They did this in the usual haphazard way: issuing emergency certifications to people with no teaching credentials. Sure, why pay a seasoned vet the amount she was making, or even close to it, when you can just emergency cert somebody, anybody, for a fraction of my salary? How hard do you think they will vet these people? Just some food for thought.

Anyhow, this meant way fewer jobs for teachers who were closing in on a decade until retirement. Once again, it seemed I had sabotaged myself. Not only was I not bringing in a salary, but we were now paying $800 per month for insurance. No, that isn't for a family, Kindreds. That was just for Tony and me. Granted, we were paying so much that we really couldn't afford the copays that went along with it. Basically, we had insurance that we didn't use because the costs were beyond our reach, just like it had been with my mom.

When I mentioned this to Tina, she was aghast. "How can it cost the price of a small mortgage to carry healthcare?"

This was the million-dollar question. Another crucial issue that no one seems to care about. Why are people okay with this? It isn't like the care has drastically improved or anything. Quite the opposite, actually. Many blame frivolous lawsuits, and they aren't completely wrong.

Again, I believe it's a combination of factors that has led to the worst possible outcomes. The pattern perpetuates and is blatantly obvious when you take off the blinders: those in positions of power have no business being there. Take our president, for example. He is ancient and very obviously mentally incapacitated. The vice president is equally useless, and this is a tough pill to swallow since she is the first female of that stature in office. The other choice is equally heinous.

Why do we even pay taxes? It's absolutely taxation without representation at this point.

September came around, but no job offers did. I went through a bout of crying because of it, then realized I couldn't change it. I prayed on it and set intentions for it, but nothing manifested.

Instead of allowing myself to buy into the spiral down, I began counting blessings. I had Kaleb and Tony. I had my three kids and my physical health. We still had a home, miraculously, and the electricity hadn't been turned off yet. It was still a massive struggle to pay everything, and some months we simply were not able to.

Something had to give. It felt as if I had spent my entire life waiting. Always searching. For what, I still didn't know. Maybe we never do figure it all out.

What I realized now, though, was that I was here. I was present. I was living and not focusing on loss and dying. I am not "fixed," probably never will be, but as Hemingway famously said, "We are all broken. That's how the light gets in."

Perhaps I am exactly where I need to be at the moment.

Chapter 25

My young adults were holding their own. Angelica and her partner have made headway, and I dared to hope the abuse has ended. Her baby daddy isn't a bad guy; he just needs the right help to overcome his issues. Aaron is currently awaiting an appointment with a new psychiatrist, who will hopefully provide him with much-needed assistance. Ella finally got her car back and has been meeting monthly with a mental health professional. Tony is Tony. He continues to grind away at work and is helpful when he can be. It has been a few months without any major issues, and I am thankful for the much-needed respite, yet apprehensive about the future.

Incredibly, the super at my old job had handed in her resignation. There were multiple criminal investigations surrounding the district, and she was, so to speak, at the helm when it all transpired. The flimsy deck of cards she had built her illusionist castle out of was finally tumbling down on her.

Possibly my largest indicator of self-growth is that I felt no joy at this. The assistant super intendent who had made his entire career there would slide into that role, as he had before. Let us remember, though, Kindreds, that this man stood idly by while the district sank to epic lows. He was no savior.

There were crickets on the job front. I think many already had someone in mind when they placed the ad, and they were just keeping it legal by going through the motions of interviewing. Finally, in October, I got a call from a local school district looking for a long-term sub. This was not an economically challenged school district. Quite the opposite, actually. I had literally gone from one end of the spectrum to another. It was enough to make your head spin.

At home, Tony and I remained together but apart. We occupied the same space, but didn't really interact unless we had to. It was uncomfortable and awkward, but neither one of us seemed poised to do something about it. And so it went on. I wasn't sleeping or eating well, my legs and back hurt all the time, and some days I honestly could not walk.

When I accepted the position at this school, I made them aware straight out of the gate that I had three days of knee injections already scheduled and I would need them off. Everyone played like it was fine by them when they were desperate to fill the position. During the first injection, the doctor hit the bone. I was crippled for two days and had to take another sick day. I hobbled through the twelve-hour day that parent-teacher conferences require, but I was hurting even when the injections were done. This was a pain so intense, I was back to throwing up.

After I had to call out again, I decided to go to the ER. Turns out, I had two bulging discs and two herniated discs. I was advised to rest for 24 hours and use lidocaine patches. A course of steroids was given, and I figured I would be right as rain. I was not. It ended up as sciatica, which is the second-worst pain I have ever felt - the first being natural labor. More missed days and feelings of ineptitude. Was I back to beating myself up, Kindreds? You bet your sweet asses I was. I limped through until winter break, but it was obvious the district was unhappy with me. I couldn't really blame them, but how could it be helped? I worked from home on the days I was out, grading papers and putting scores in the electronic gradebook. The class was six weeks behind when I took over. There was a lot to catch up on. I was no slug. I just couldn't walk.

"Now that your brain is healing, your body is breaking down" said a quiet, familiar voice in my head. I pushed it aside.

Possibly the best news is that Kaleb was emerging. He still wasn't saying sentences, but he was saying words, phrases, singing along to songs and babbling incessantly. It was lovely to listen to his little sounds as he ran around the house playing. Kaleb had started attending class through the local intermediate unit, and it was helping. Their whole little family seemed well-adjusted and more content. It made me hopeful that they would finally turn from the constant bickering that eventually brings a blow-up with accompanying violence and trauma. Ain't nobody got time for that.

Conversely, Aaron was a sinking ship again. I had gotten him on my insurance, and he went to a new psychiatrist. He seemed a bit better at first, but he apparently decided to stop the meds. I don't know why-hell, he probably doesn't either. This, of course, led to a descent from which he may never entirely return.

It began when he broke his phone the weekend before. We were all up at the cabin, and it hit the wood floor and shattered. We had fixed this phone umpteen times, and honestly, I didn't think it could be fixed. He was training for a new job and still didn't have a car, so he was stuck with SEPTA, and they suck, as he quickly learned. He ended up stranded, having to walk for 10 miles. He came home agitated, which I get, but he quickly became aggressive. Kaleb was asleep upstairs, so we tried to calm Aaron down. He wouldn't or couldn't. My money is on the latter. Things got out of hand when Ella turned to warn Tony and me:

"This is how he looked when he attacked me. Be careful, guys."

As she walked by Aaron, he started screaming rabidly at her. Ella returned fire. It got ugly fast, and Aaron lunged for Ella. Tony and I pulled him back. I am much shorter than Aaron, so I had my hands around his throat and shoulder, pulling him away. I had my elbows leaning into his collarbone, hoping he would stop. He kept pushing forward, his throat getting squeezed. As Tony put his back into it, Aaron stood. I still had my hands around his throat. I looked in his eyes and thought about how, in that moment, I wanted to choke the disease out of him. Obviously, I never would, and you can't ever rid him of the illness, but I am keeping it real and owning my truth. He was trying to get physical with his sister again, and this time right in front of us. We sent Ella to scoop up Kaleb and go to her room and lock the door.

We tried to talk him down, but Aaron just kept getting more agitated and aggressive. Tony sent me upstairs, and I went and hid out with Ella and the baby. I don't know how Kaleb did it, but he slept through the entire ordeal. Long story short, because let's face it, Kindreds, the trauma and drama don't ever seem to end around these parts, Tony took Aaron to the local hotel and put him up for the night. I came home from work the next day to find him here, of course, irrational. A friend called my phone for him, and I made the mistake of letting him answer it. This dude was wackier than Aaron if at all possible. He told my son to get out because I was "a clone." I told Aaron to hang up, and things got uglier. He ended up calling 911 on me using my own phone. Ironic, no?

My biggest mistake was telling Aaron I was so scared of him the night before, I considered sleeping with a gun. Both Tony and I are responsible, registered gun owners. We have a gun locker in our room that no one has access to but us. We are both so mentally drained and just not functioning on a level akin to being responsible enough to operate firearms. Formerly, I didn't carry unless I was going to the cabin alone. Tony used to be a regular, all-day carry guy. As I said before, it's ironic how you know your limits even when you don't know anything else. Purely defense weapons, they remained under lock and key - even to us.

When I use the term 'responsible,' that does not mean we just locked the guns away. We had joined a Field and Stream Club when our children were younger. We regularly took them there, and Tony taught them gun safety. They enjoyed it. They respected the procedures, the practices and the pistols. Much like me, they never took to it, but my point is that they learned how to handle a firearm responsibly, and that is necessary if a home is to house guns.

As previously mentioned, my father was a Marine. He collected guns after his discharge. He would go to a little cabin in Maine with my Godfather every winter to hunt bear. My dad got one, and the obligatory "baby on a bear skin rug" photo session took place. My mom gave me the only remaining photo when she downsized. At some point as a youngster, I took a marker and colored baby Jen's eyes black. It is creepy, yet suitable. I still have it.

Anyhow, Dad didn't keep his guns locked up; they were hanging right at the top of the cellar stairs. Oddly enough, this was where we hung our school backpacks every day. We never touched them, though. We, kids, would ogle, ahh and then move about our business. It was a learned behavior. We knew they were not for our consumption, although we watched Bugs Bunny maim Elmer Fudd almost daily. Plus, the Road Runner blowing up the Coyote. Common sense seemed to run amok back then - now, not so much.

When the police finally came, I just wanted the ground to swallow me. I was so utterly exhausted and drained to the core that I honestly didn't think I had it in me to make sense. About seven showed up since a firearm was reported. I get it, but the one dude was a total narcissistic tool. He reminded me of that psychiatrist who barked out questions yet didn't wait for answers. I was starting to feel way too overwhelmed. A buzzing began in my ears.

"Please no!" my mind screamed.

This was not the time for a panic attack. I tried to focus on one thing - my Jeep at the top of the driveway - as a way of grounding myself. I started up my breathing routine as Tina had taught me.

At this exact time, two negative things happened: Aaron came out the back door to greet three cops, and the previously mentioned douchebag started eyeballing me while I was trying to bring myself down with my breathing. It was almost as if he thought I might be on drugs and freaking out because of his "police presence" (I use that term very loosely.)

Determined not to lose my shit in front of the crap cop, I instead focused on what was transpiring up the driveway with Aaron and his trio. He was sitting on the back bumper of my Jeep, looking smug as a bug. Little did he realize, these small-town kiddie cops would eat him alive if given half the chance. They knew he was mentally ill and didn't give a fig. Officer Offensive would look like a hero if he took down some local gun owners trapped in a family dispute. It didn't matter that both Tony and I were registered gun owners, registered voters, and, not too long ago, were pillars of the local softball program that they, the police force, sponsored.

Thankfully, Ella pulled up, fresh out of work, looking forward to a Friday evening. I saw her incredulous look as she slowly drove past our house, navigating the multiple cop cars. She found a spot and speed walked up our street.

Given the abbreviated version of what had happened, Officer Ogre barked out some stuff and turned on his heel to saunter up my driveway towards Aaron and his little crowd of law enforcement. Almost as if on cue, a young black cop dressed in undercover clothes turned and came down the drive to Ella and me.

"Hey, Ella," he said, advancing towards us.

"Hi Jaylen," she responded cooly.

Why was I not surprised that my daughter was on a first-name basis with the local police? This entire situation was so surreal, anything seemed plausible.

When it was all said and done, Aaron was made to leave the property. His buddy was picking him up. Major Blow Hard pontificated for a few more, telling me to go to Crozer and get a judge to order him to get help. Like it was just that easy. I was crying at this point. Sargent Shit Head gave me a nasty look and asked why I was crying.

"Is he for real?" a familiar voice in my brain asked.

At this point, I was beyond fried and utterly flabbergasted that this so-called "servant of society" could be that out of touch and unfeeling.

"He definitely is not a parent," that voice piped up again.

Honestly, who cared? My taxes paid his salary if we wanted to be real about it, and I had lived here for over twenty years. This government mule could kiss my Irish ass was my immediate thought. Yet I was old and wise enough to know that is not the approach to take. I told him that having my son forcibly removed hurt beyond words, and I was concerned about the firearm report since I was a public-school teacher.

Corporal Condescending's response was about what I expected. He reproached me loudly. At this point, Aaron was being escorted out with some bags he had hastily packed. He looked like he wanted to kill me.

"Thanks, Mom," he spat at me as he strode by.

Just when you think your heart can't break anymore, it does. I began sobbing, and the guy who knew Ella stayed close, as did a young female officer and another officer about my age. They offered words of support and advice on getting immediate help for Aaron.

"I thought you might be causing trouble," teased the young black undercover officer, turning towards Ella.

She blushed, and I looked him over. He was cute - dressed in a black concert tee, denim jacket, construction boots, and jeans so tight they paid homage to the eighties. I watched as he walked away and climbed into an unmarked SUV that was so obviously a fuzz, why bother with the disguise?

At that exact moment, all of their radios went off. Apparently, there was a shooting at the local pizza joint. As they sprinted towards their respective vehicles, I called out a thank you.

"I guess that dude was done waiting on his pie," or some such cheese I added over my shoulder while Ella dragged me up the driveway.

In my defense, this food joint was notorious for screwing up meal orders. By all means, that does not mean I condone violence. As I have attempted to illustrate, my mind was once again dancing on the edge of the precipice. So, this seemed like appropriate banter, but we all know it isn't.

"And how many well-known people have made similar mistakes and been branded as unacceptable?" My inner voice was truly my mirror - cancel culture is ridiculous, unpredictable and unnecessary. We all make mistakes. As Jesus said, "Let thee without sin cast the first stone."

So long as we learn from those mistakes, we are on the right path. It's all an evolution. That's the end game, although many think otherwise. There are not enough words in my vernacular to accurately display my gratitude for my mental breakdown. While I would never choose to repeat it, the knowledge, introspectiveness, and general empathy I gained in hell have allowed me to grow as a person. While it is a heck of a way to forge forward, I trust the process. Plus, I firmly believe my ancestors are pulling for me and cheering me on. The phrase "God willing" now has a new meaning.

Back in the present, Aaron's ride was the crazy cat that told him I was a clone. Birds of a feather tend to flock together. Until push comes to shove, literally. Aaron called me a few nights later. It was raining like the dickens. Apparently, he and his disturbed host got into a fight, and he got tossed. Here he was wandering miles from the house with his bags in the cold and dark while it poured down icy rain. I offered to come get him. He told me he needed "to walk off the anger."

While I was thankful his pride didn't get in the way of his reaching out to me, I lamented that lessons like these need to be harshly learned. Why was I perceived as the enemy time and again when I was just trying to help? Both at home and at my former job. It was more than I could wrap my measly brain around.

In the end, I paid for an Uber to take Aaron to that same hotel Tony had put him up in. I went to the local Wawa and bought him hot soup and such. When I dropped it off at the hotel for him, I decided just to leave it at the desk for him to pick up. I knew Aaron couldn't face me right now, and to be honest, I didn't want to see him either.

Once again, there isn't a sufficient word in my vocabulary to illustrate how horrific it is to be afraid of your own child. I still loved Aaron; nothing would ever change that. Yet, I had no idea how to help him. He was going to end up in jail for attacking someone he didn't know.

"Would you rather that or a mental institution?"

"Hello darkness, my old friend," I sang into the night as I drove home from the hotel. I pondered the question my inner voice had raised. It no longer mattered which one - the voices were one and the same, I had realized. Just the Yin and Yang, the light and the dark, the dual existence of a Gemini. The realization began to occur to me that I had shattered into so many pieces at this point that they no longer fit together. I was a puzzle that could not be solved. Sort of like Humpty Dumpty, never to be put together again.

"No longer whole," sighed my inner voice sadly.

"Forever broken," added the other one.

"That is how the light gets in," I thought, quoting Hemingway again.

"What if we are all just dead already?" I wondered aloud. "And this is just one giant charade? Like a play being acted out." The idea was terrifying, and even I must admit, insane.

"The Matrix " the voices declared triumphantly.

"Like the book *Under the Dome,*" I mused. "We are just a huge science fair project thrown together by some superior race."

These thoughts did nothing to warm me as I arrived home and stepped out into the freezing cold rain driven by a strong North Eastern wind. I stood in the driveway, face turned up towards the stars. The freezing droplets mixed with my own tears. I was cold to my core, and it had nothing to do with this wicked weather. All I wanted to do was shed these soaking wet clothes and crawl into bed with the covers over my head.

The next morning, I let Tony know about Aaron and what had transpired the night before.

"We can't afford to keep putting him up in hotels, Jen," Tony stated.

"I know," I lamented.

"But he can't come here," we both said in unison.

We gazed at each other intently. It was good to be on the same wavelength again, even if it was trauma-driven. As much as neither one of us wanted to do it, we decided to try and 302 him.

It was a quick ride to Crozer Medical, which was currently the only place accepting intake for mental illness. We arrived before either of us felt ready, but in truth, we never would be. This is what we had been dreading ever since his first mental crisis. My feet were as heavy as my heart, and I stumbled up to the locked door to ring the bell.

A security officer opened the door, and we explained why we were there. He informed us that only one person at a time is allowed in. I looked at Tony, and he shook his head. Turning to the guard, I told him it would be me. He instructed me to give my purse and phone to my husband. Nothing was allowed in except me. I gave Tony my belongings, and he offered me a weak smile of support. I turned to follow the guard through the large steel door. There was a second security door, and he buzzed us in.

It was dark inside. As my eyes adjusted to the low lights, I glanced around. There was a waiting room with a few plastic chairs secured to the floor. SpongeBob was playing on the television. The guard sat down at his post, which was behind me and to the left. A nurse approached the window and asked what I wanted. I explained the situation and added that the police told me this was my best course of action to help him. She gave me the paperwork to fill out. I went about the task of filling it out. Since I had a pen that could be used as a weapon, I had to stand there in front of the guard to fill it all out. Said guard took turns between trolling on his phone and laughing at SpongeBob playing on the TV. His laughter was so out of place in this dungeon that I kept glancing over at him every time he belted out his deep, belly giggles.

There was a door next to him. I kept detecting movement behind it, but the lights were turned off in there, so I couldn't see where the door led. As I wrapped up the request for a 302, the nurse returned and reviewed it.

"I don't know that this will be enough for the judge to approve it, but hang tight, and we will see," she said.

"How could attacking people multiple times not be enough?" I wondered to myself.

As I watched, the nurse went to a fax machine and fed my paperwork through. I stood waiting. After a while, I started to gaze around in earnest. I wanted to see what this place was about since my son could likely end up a resident. The furniture - what little there was - screamed 1970 at me. In fact, so did the flooring, the faded blue walls, and the fluorescent lights that kept blinking. When was the last time this place was updated?

It looked like something out of a horror movie. Once again, it was very obvious that resources are not being directed to the right places.

Movement behind that same door caught my eye again. As I strained to see, I realized a little girl was standing at the small window in the door. She was looking right at me. I felt a chill go through my body. This child had very pale skin and big, dark eyes. Her eyes were expressionless as she watched me watching her. She almost resembled a ghost; the lack of lighting made her pale skin glow like the full moon on a dark night.

"Why would they lock a little girl away in here?" my inner voice asked.

It was then that I heard a woman's voice behind that same door. She was moaning and groaning. Then she screamed that her phone had been taken. The little girl disappeared.

I could hear shuffling noises now, and the guard finally got off his rear end to look into the room through the little window. Whatever he saw satisfied him, and he went back to watching SpongeBob. Horrified, my mind went into overtime thinking up situations that could potentially lead to a juvenile being locked away in here. The most reasonable thing I came up with is that she may have attacked the police or ambulance personnel when they came to take her mom. Whatever it was, I felt deeply sorry for this little nameless girl with the crazy mom.

At this point, the nurse was answering a phone call. I saw her glance at me and then look down, speaking in a hushed tone. The hair on my neck and arms stood up. I glanced at the door, and sure enough, little Miss Grim was back. She was watching me intently again. The window to the nurses' station opened (most likely bulletproof glass), and my name was called. I took a few steps forward, and the nurse handed me back my paperwork.

"Sorry, hon. It was denied. The judge doesn't think he meets the criteria for commitment right now based on your report," the nurse said.

"So attacking a family member isn't enough? What does he have to do - kill someone before he qualifies for help?" I asked incredulously.

She repeated her apologies, and I thanked her for her time. It isn't her fault the system is so broken. As I turned towards the guard, I was face -to-face with the little white ghost. I noticed she had long brown hair that hung in greasy clumps. A Hello Kitty headband was holding the worst of it back from her small, moon-shaped face. A pain tore through my heart, and bile began to rise in my throat. I followed the guard to the exit and glanced back at her once more. I gave her a tight, tiny smile and a quick wave. I just wanted her to know that she was seen. She mattered.

"I'll see you tonight in my nightmares, kid" I mumbled to myself.

The sunlight was blinding when I stepped out into it. I just stood blinking - I literally could see nothing but sunspots dancing before my eyes. It was hard to breathe, and the bile was coming back up my esophagus. Tony hopped out and helped me get in the car. We headed towards home, and I filled Tony in on what had happened. I left the little girl out, though. She was my secret to keep.

When we returned home, Aaron called to tell me he was moving into his new place, which he had been waiting for. This was good news, if he could just hold it together long enough to let it be. That night, much like any other, I prayed for my kids, but this time I fell asleep praying for Aaron. So many prayers. Maybe they kept the little ghost away, because thankfully, she did not visit me in my slumber that night or any other.

"It means you are now officially desensitized to trauma."

Once upon a time, this would have given me pause. Not anymore, however. I wasn't just desensitized, I was dead inside. My joy and zest for life had not been thus restored. Yes, there were good times. I loved being with Kaleb. He made me laugh like no other. He was so silly and lovable. Plus, work was good, although I really missed having my own classroom. The staff were kind, the kids were humorous, and, for the most part, well-behaved. They liked to learn. There, of course, were the jokesters and some bullying, but nothing on the massive scale of dissociation and violence like at the old gig.

So what gives? Why am I just existing still? I wanted to go back to wonder and amusement, and warmth. The isolation I had put myself into seems to have had lasting effects. I am no longer comfortable in a room full of adults. Yet I thrive in a room full of students. Go figure.

It was easy to retain my wonder about nature, but I just didn't bother to share it with anyone anymore. That is to say, I was forever the one pointing out the flowers, birds, clouds, and stars. I 'm still in awe of these things; I just keep them to myself. I keep a lot to myself, honestly, anymore. It felt safer. I was content to sit and listen to Ella and Tony banter at night when we all got home from work. We still watched Kaleb three nights a week, and that gave me much-needed dopamine. I smile pretty much the entire time I am with him. He keeps me going.

That alone was not enough, though. I still felt as if I had no purpose. Tony didn't understand when I tried to tell him how I felt.

"Of course you have a purpose, Jen. You are Kaleb's Nonma, and a mother to Ella, Aaron and Ang. You are my wife, and I love you. We all love you. Why isn't that enough?" he asked bitterly.

Why indeed. His words made me feel like an ungrateful asshole, so I dropped it. No one got it. Something was missing. Some vital ingredient, but I will be damned if I know what it is I am searching for.

My career means a lot to me, so I acknowledge that it is definitely part of it. I was subbing and desperately needed a contract to ride out my next eleven years until retirement. I missed not only having my own space but also the camaraderie of the school staff. I also missed delving deep into content with students and witnessing that "lightbulb moment" when it all comes together. As a sub, I was in different classrooms every day, not making real connections; they were all fleeting. Plus, I was teaching a wide range of subjects, not just my discipline. What I really think is that I am still grieving. I will forever be grieving not only for my ma, but also for my son. It is horrible to mourn someone who isn't dead yet, but I do. The old, easygoing Aaron was gone forever. The quiet, smart, studious, respectful, happy, lovable Aaron was dead. He was never coming back. So I mourned. I mourned deep in my soul and my heart and my mind. I could not fix this for him. He was already complaining about his meds and such. It was only a matter of time before he stopped taking them entirely again. And we all know what happens when he ceases medication.

Furthermore, Tony and I have often discussed what will happen to him when we are gone. It's grossly unfair to expect his sisters to have to care for him. I have always hoped he would be solid enough to get by on his own, and that the girls would just check in on him. Or take him to dinner, whatever. But he is so far from being okay, I couldn't fathom any other scenario when we are dead and gone. We did not want him to be the crazy guy wandering around town, muttering to himself. You know the one who sometimes gets irrationally angry for no good reason? Most towns have one. They could be ex-military or just mentally ill. Maybe down on their luck or fallen on hard times. Perhaps an addict, or an ex-addict. Or they could be my son. Or my brother, come to think of it.

And I wonder why I have lost my joy and zest for life? Why indeed.

Chapter 26

Spring that year was cold and rainy. Teachers despise indoor recess and rightly so. The students need time outside to burn off energy and breathe fresh air. Free play is so undervalued in public education. Then we wonder why social skills are lacking. At least this district did it right. The elementary school where I was ending my year is a really nice place to work. I had accepted a summer ESY position with this district, and they had paid to emergency-certify me in Special Ed. I was looking forward to being a learning support, because that was very similar to the position I had held at my old district. Things were starting to look up.

If we were to broach financials, Tony and I would probably agree that we have made strides. There were many more hurdles to conquer, but we were working on it. However, I will never understand how two years in hell set us back ten. Tony was sincerely unhappy at his job. He came home angry and aggravated most nights. When he told Ella and me why, we got it; this was why Ella had recently left that company and found a dispatcher job elsewhere. Tony would be the next one out the door.

However, it was May, and we were quickly approaching summer. Tony wanted his paid summer vacation, and who could blame him? His company reminded me much of my old gig - epic dysfunction ran through every level. What it comes down to at the end of the day is that those good at their job are rewarded with more to do, so we can carry the burden of those who just want to skate through the workday. This just goes to show that it isn't feasible on any front. It wasn't at my old school, and it isn't at Tony's Heating and Cooling company. Self-interest ran at an all-time high, as did laziness and entitlement. Personally, I am of the mind that this is also a post-pandemic phenomenon. There is no loyalty, no recognition or reward for doing the right thing. Corporate greed was the model, and the peasants followed suit. You know, Kindreds - the Sheeple.

Given, evolution and growth are the goals, there is a price to pay. As there always is. The price this time is "The Realizing." The realizing that the world is most likely beyond saving. The realizing that humans are inherently flawed. The realization that no one truly has the energy or capacity to care like we, as a race, used to. The old Queen song put it best when Bowie joined in and sang "That's the terror of knowing what this world is about…" Sometimes I am that friend screaming, "Let me out."

It's a burden, this "opening of your third eye." I see and feel things that most people could, but they float by with their faces stuck in their phones. And that's exactly what is desired by …. the 1%, the Illuminati, the Dark State, whatever you want to term it. I know it exists, and I am helpless to change it, so I do what we all do I ignore it until I can't in the deep, dark recesses of the night when sleep eludes me and prayers have deserted me. Why are we like this? Why do we exploit and hurt each other?

According to the studies I conducted leading up to my Master's degree, this is a learned behavior. So how do we change it? Oh, that's right, we can't. It's not in the country's best interest for everyone to get along. The media can attest to that. We collectively can't get our shit together enough to direct money and resources to the things that really matter: Mental health, education, health care, the growing debt, the border crisis and the list goes on. I have stated it all here before, yet nothing changes. How then, can I "Be The Change?" I have written earlier about hope being a necessary ingredient. I still think my missing piece is self-fulfillment. I needed something of my own.

Last time I endeavored to do that, I ended up having a nervous breakdown. So I waited. I prayed for it to be made clear to me what I was to do. What is my calling?

Tony would tell me Kaleb was, and yes, I loved him more than any other human. However, I did not possess a degree in early childhood education, so I did not know how to help him. We just sang together a lot because he would sing songs and speak infrequently; he just wouldn't straight-up talk to people. He didn't have the capacity or, perhaps, the desire to converse. He preferred his own little world, and hell, who could blame him? All I could do was love him intensely, and that was one thing I was still good at. He gave me hugs and kisses and would snuggle his face into my neck. I made him feel safe and warm, and that, in itself, was a blessing for us both.

However, I will not be a full-time Nonma this summer for the first time since he was born. I will miss it incredibly. Instead, I will be teaching in this superior school district, trying to prove my worth. That was okay, I needed a challenge. Angelica was in a good enough space that she would work her schedule, and I would just continue to have Kaleb after school until bedtime. I was utterly grateful for that.

Memorial Day weekend was upon us. I had been crying for the past few weeks. It didn't help that I drove by the cemetery where my mom was buried every day to and from work. It was a difficult time for me; first, Easter, then Mother's Day, and finally my birthday. Those are all special days that I have always spent with Mom, and they all occurred within 4 weeks. It was like emotional overdrive. Yet, the ache no longer took my breath away. Now it was just a constant companion, sort of like an abscess that refused to close and heal.

My youngest brother and his wife were coming to the cabin for the weekend, and I was really excited for their visit. I did not get to see them nearly enough, and they were my only tie to Mom now. Baby bro was the only one left from the original gang. The bloodline. That in itself made me sad. We used to be a large family that got together frequently and had fun. It was all gone now, all the good ones were gone. I knew it was up to me to forge forward and create new memories. Everyone says that is the best way to honor your people. I wanted Mom to be proud of me, wherever she was.

So Kindreds, as you can see, we had settled into our new life whether we wanted to or not. Time marches on. I held tight to the belief that I would see my mother again in whatever comes next. That kept me going. I still talked to Mom out loud every day. It keeps me sane. Those drives home though …. They wrecked me some days when there was traffic, and I was stuck sitting right outside of where she and my dad were buried. It made me feel so alone. Of course, I wasn't when I got home, but that is how I felt -very alone and tired beyond weary. Only orphans will understand this, and I acknowledge that. It is sort of like being in a room full of people but being invisible. Unfortunately, most of us will know this pain someday. For you, my Kindreds, I hope it is far off into the future, for you will be forever changed.

This change was obvious in my youngest brother. I could not imagine losing my mom at his age, and that humbled me. It was time to acknowledge others' grief. I finally had the brain power to entertain that. What an amazing legacy she left, though. I am still in awe of how her closest friend has kept in touch. She feels the unending void, too.

We had a grand time that weekend, even if it was too busy to do everything we wanted to. My brother and his wife left on Sunday afternoon. Tony had hung tough, but didn't look good. When inquired of, he stated he "didn't feel right." That afternoon, we landed in the emergency room. Tony had kidney stones.

His amount of pain was incredible. He had the sweats but was freezing. His legs and feet vibrated the entire cabin, but he couldn't control it. Tony was in the worst shape I had seen him in. Considering we were coming up on our 31st wedding anniversary next month, that spoke volumes. The poor guy passed one in the hospital, and was sent home harboring the other. He was advised to drink 120 oz. of water a day to help him pass it.

That was an insane amount to have to drink if you weren't planning on spending the day in the bathroom. He somehow managed it.

It was advised to follow up with our family doctor, so Tony made an appointment. When he arrived home, he was flabbergasted. The doc had looked over all the imaging and tests the hospital had done, and he was of the mind that Tony had kidney cancer! The staff mentioned that something showed up on his imaging that he should follow up on, but we assumed it was a cyst, since Tony has had them before. Never in a million years did I entertain the thought that it was a tumor they saw!

Needless to say, we were both thrown for a loop. Tony went for more tests the following day. He scheduled an MRI with the script the doctor had given him. The first opening they had was a week away. So we waited and agonized. No, it was not lost on me that I had wanted out of this thing called life last year, and now I was facing losing Tony. Was this a punishment? Because it sure seemed that way. I was not trying to make this about me, Kindreds. So please don't think I am. I just felt that this was God's way of showing me how precious life was, and how wrong I was to take it for granted.

Either way you sliced it, we were once again eating a big, old, shit sandwich. We had grinded and clawed back from the brink of bankruptcy, and now that we had finally gained considerable ground, this was thrown at us. I knew better than to wish it all away, because why bury my head in the sand? Inaction would change nothing. Sure, we both hoped and prayed it was a cyst. Yet the way the doctor had spoken about it, I was fairly certain this was the real deal. The Big C.

When Tony asked our doctor why he was talking about treatment options when we aren't even sure what it is, Doc replied, "I am just trying to soften the blow for you."

Honestly, I didn't know how to handle any of this, and the one person I wanted to lean on was Mom. But we all know that isn't possible. Instead, I stopped at the cemetery on my way home from work. I sat on the grass facing her headstone and just cried. I didn't say much; it was all tears. Silent tears, too. There was no yelling or moaning this time. Tears flowed from my eyes and slid down my face, soaking the front of my shirt. I sat like this for a while, then began calming down. It was very peaceful here, at my mom's final resting place. I didn't feel any closer to her, but I did experience comfort. She had sent me more signs today - numbers again. On the clock, quite literally and figuratively.

It was one of those days when I ran from class to class, covering teachers' meetings. I don't wear a watch, so typically I just check the classroom clock to make sure I am where I need to be on time. The first time I checked, it was 11:11. "Make a wish," I whispered under my breath.

When I looked at the clock that afternoon, it was 1:11, then 2:22 and finally 3:33. Odd, no? I thought so. What did it mean? To me, it was confirmation of what I suspected was true (that Tony had cancer), and it was meant to let me know I am not alone in this.

At least that is how I viewed it.

After the MRI, it took a few days for the phone call. I couldn't believe our good fortune - Tony didn't have cancer! It was some sort of rare cyst that was filled with blood and mimicked that awful disease, but Tony was in the clear! I was so grateful and thankful. The prayers of thanksgiving flowed from my lips that night.

In June, the school year ended, and so did my paycheck, until the following week, when ESY (Extended School Year) started. From a financial standpoint, things were rough. We had two of Tony's nieces graduate, and then his nephew got married on the 4th of July weekend. We rented a cottage down in Maryland where the nuptials were being held. All of these extras were straining us, but "family comes first" is my motto. The nephew being wed is the son of Tony's brother, who had passed away shortly after my mom. This was not a wedding to be missed. Everyone needed to rally around and support them. I can't even imagine how hard it was for them to focus on the positives while missing him so much. His void was definitely felt. The groom wore a photo pendant pin of his father on his tuxedo. My sister-in-law danced with her brother, which was sweet, but it should have been her and her husband joyfully celebrating together. Alas, that could never be again. She is amazing and held it together throughout. I truly admire her resolve.

We all had a good time despite the heat. Aaron was doing well. He was more like his old self, and that made my heart soar. I made sure to tell him how awesome he was doing and added, "whatever it is you have going on, please keep doing it." I figure if I am telling him when he needs to clean up his act, I also need to tell him when he is doing great. As always, I am cautiously optimistic that this time he will carry through with his meds and appointments. Pray, wish and hope. It's still better than panic attacks and paranoia.

As July wore on, I kept busy with teaching special needs students at ESY and babysitting Kaleb. The extended school year ended when July did. That meant I would no longer have a paycheck after the second week of August. Yes, Kindreds, I was back to that again. I couldn't continue being a building sub; I simply couldn't afford the pay cut that came with it. All I wanted to do was help children learn how to read. Why was that so difficult to obtain? It's not like I am asking to hit the lottery, although it would be a Godsend. I was once again at a major crossroads, and I didn't know what to do. I had applied for quite a few jobs, but again heard nothing back. It was definitely demoralizing. I prayed nightly for something positive to happen in the job arena.

Since my prayers remain unanswered, I have expanded my job search beyond Delaware County public schools. Did I want to spend an extra 45 minutes driving to and from work? Of course not, traffic gave me road rage anymore. Yet, I would do it if that's what it took to stay financially solvent. The way I looked at it, I could catch up on podcasts and such while driving. This was a change, too - instead of being bitter about it, I changed how I looked at it. The old Jen would have been pissed and indignant. She would have ranted and raved about all the gas money wasted and time burned. The new Jen rolled with the punches and found ways to adapt. Why spend energy getting worked up about what I cannot change? There isn't enough energy to last all day anyhow. It was another dreaded thing about aging: the lack of energy and rest. The lack of sleep and relaxation. The '50s were like gearing up for the last big push. Retirement is looming. The clock is ticking. So, I kept looking and applying.

Speaking of aging, I had to wonder whether I was being passed over because of it. I was 54 now, and it amazed even me. Why hire someone who is in the last decade or so of teaching when you can take on a brand-new teacher, fresh out of college? One that you can pay a lot less for, and mold into what you want. It sounds far-fetched, but ageism is most certainly a thing. Just look at Hollywood and its practices. Roles dry up for even starlets eventually.

My next move was to apply to a charter school. I didn't want to do this, but I needed a solid paycheck. Plus, I can make a difference wherever I go. I am just that way. What I really wanted was to keep my pension intact, but I wasn't being given any other options. The district I had been subbing for all year had a Reading Specialist opening, and I applied. That was in June, and I haven't heard a peep from them, although I am still teaching there. I guess those missed days at the beginning of the school year really hurt me, far more than just physically.

Chapter 27

While my little world was sort of coming together, the rest of it was falling apart. Ukraine was still at war with Russia and attempting to gain entry to NATO for defense. Biden and Trump had their debate, and it was both amusing and dismaying. It was basically a pissing contest. They even argued about their golf scores! It was very obvious that good ol' Joe had dementia or some sort of brain issue related to age. The dude was as old as dirt. It showed - he couldn't follow a logical thought without trailing off and ending with something entirely different. He looked like a corpse and made about as much sense. Trump, on the other hand, was his typical narcissistic self, although even he managed to tone it down a bit. At the end of the day, they are both just little men; boys embroiled in a dick swinging contest. I trust neither of them, and am abhorred that these two morons are our only viable choices. I was torn - I was getting tired of voting for a third party when no one else is. We needed a grassroots movement to catch fire - sort of like it did in the '60s. No one seems up to the task, though. It was a sad state of affairs for sure. The democrats were certain to find a replacement candidate for Biden. That man can't run an errand, let alone an entire country. Makes you wonder who has been running the show for the past four years.

All I know is inflation is through the goddamn roof, and the middle class is being eked out. Healthcare is worse than ever, and our taxes are insanely high, especially when you consider what we get in return. American middle-class families are not built for Biden's economy. Yet, the other mainstream choice was equally dismal.

"God help us," I prayed daily. We, as a country, are so far removed from what we once were. It was enough to drive me down into despair when I allowed myself to ponder it. Our choices boiled down to the Fool or the Felon.

Our family settled into an uneasy pattern, but at least it was a routine. Tony and I desperately wanted to sell the house and get out from under the burden of this crushing mortgage payment. We were constantly behind on everything, and it was hurting our credit score. Yet we were unable to pay for the improvements needed to sell and get a good price. See the conundrum?

We puttered on through our new, ill-fitting existence. Tony had used up his sick time for the kidney stone debacle and follow-up testing. I spent Fridays following up with doctors' appointments, running errands and looking online for jobs. Halfway through July, our vacation started. The kids were unable to make it this year because everyone is hurting from the economy. The over blown prices eat up any extras, such as fun. Tony and I rarely had time alone, and we both desperately needed some downtime, so this vacation, while different from any other, was a welcome respite. Tony and I didn't do much; we puttered around the cabin, doing cleaning and maintenance. We watched a ton of movies, read books, did yard work and lounged by the pool. Even our dogs sensed the wind down. They lay around and weren't up our butts like they typically are.

Previously, I wrote about how disconnected I was from politics. Tony had always been into it, but even he was distancing himself from the farce our presidency is. On Saturday afternoon, Tony was napping in his recliner, and I was sitting on the porch with the dogs. While I was trolling on my phone, an article caught my eye. Apparently, there had been an attempt on Trump's life. I saw the picture of him pumping his fist while blood flowed from his ear. I immediately knew he had been grazed and prayed that no one else was hurt. This had just happened, and there were scant few details available. I shot a text to Tony so he would see it when he woke up. I put down my phone and thought intently on what this could mean. Who would do such a thing? I can not for the life of me comprehend how someone could place that little value on a human life.

Never one to buy into the hype, I stayed off social media for the remainder of the day. I was unsure what the national reaction would be, but I was not up to reading the dirty details and accompanying asinine remarks. Tony awoke and stuck his head out the door to tell me, "They shot Trump." I told him I knew, and that's when our phones went off. Ang chimed into our "fam chat" text group and stated: "They are trying to martyr him. It's an election ploy."

One had to wonder, given Trump's low polling scores lately. Who knew? We never would. The ironic part is that, as far-fetched as this sounds, it is possible because our world has gone as crazy as I.

Fortunately, both parties condemned what transpired. Biden, for once, made sense when he addressed the press. I was glad that the two mainstream parties agreed on something, anything. One would have to be an absolute ass of the worst kind to applaud this act, yet I had no doubt some did. That's how far down humanity has sunk. I hope that this might unite the country a bit and not push us further apart. Honestly, it would not take much more to tear us asunder. The divide in America was huge. I was seriously uneasy, though. It felt as if this was a harbinger of doom. A catalyst that will place motions in action that cannot be reversed.

In the following days, more details were made public. One man was killed, and two others were injured. A finger-pointing contest began between agencies: who failed, who should have done what, and so on. Whatever the reasons, it was blatantly clear that security lagged.

In addition, the alleged shooter's parents were licensed therapists. How then did they not realize that their son needed help? I am not judging - any parent who loses a child has my utmost sympathy. Personally, I don't think I could carry on after burying a child. Yet, I wondered if they were just too close to the situation to make an educated decision on mental health services for their son. People who had gone to high school with the shooter claim that he was a loner. He was bullied and isolated. That definitely fits the pattern of those who carry out these horrific acts of violence.

What didn't fit was that his parents were involved in mental health services, so how did he fall through the cracks? I would be willing to wager that he rarely saw his own school counselor for whatever reason. The system had failed this young adult, so he took his anger and frustration out on the system. I am by no means condoning what he did, but I just know that we should be doing better for people like him.

It would certainly be interesting to see how the voters reacted to this situation. I might actually dare to peek at the most recent polls this week. With roughly three and a half months to go until the election, I vowed not to watch network news. I would get my news by researching and locating the truth, which usually lies somewhere between what CNN and FOX say. America was not the only country in a mess, though. Ukraine was still defending against Russia.

Meanwhile, North Korea apparently executed 30 middle school students for watching South Korean TV! Speaking of which, the dictator/despot of North Korea wants more nukes. Israel and Palestine bomb each other daily, and we supply weapons to both Israel and Ukraine. Talk about a worldwide mess.

My dreams, which were rare, reflected this global turmoil… Sorrowful, sad dreams in which I was always cast out. I was dreaming of apocalyptic scenes and of impossible situations to escape from. In most of these dreams, the thread was how helpless and invisible I am. I would talk and try to help people, but everyone ignores me and continues on. It was distressing to the point that Tony told me I was hollering and crying in my sleep.

There was still that feeling of waiting for something, but now it seemed dire. I still don't know what it is, but I sensed it wasn't positive, more like ominous. Perhaps it was just my overactive imagination coupled with anxiety. I had recently weaned myself off another anxiety medication, so some lows seemed reasonable. I was now taking only one depression medication. While I may very well end up on it for life, I was still proud of my dwindling medication list. This alone made me feel more in control of my own life than I had in quite some time.

However, the circus seemed to be just gearing up: Biden pulled out of the presidential race. His VP would now be the Democratic candidate. She was no better than Biden, and I was afraid the Sheeple would follow suit and elect her. The border was one thing she was tasked with during Biden's four years in office. I don't think she even visited the border, which was just as well. Who needed more media shots of a female dressed up crying at the fence of a detention center? Seriously, though, if the border is any indication of her work ethic and ability, then voters should be angry. The mess at the border is getting worse, and while on her watch. What else would she fail to do as the first female president?

With all of this swirling in my head, I was feeling pretty down again. It didn't help that I was soon going to be unemployed. There was a constant feeling of powerlessness and stress. We were going under without a second paycheck, yet I could not force people to hire me. I prayed on it, cried over it, but nothing happened. While I wished that there was someone to talk to about my insecurities, there wasn't. Jocelyn just didn't get me anymore. She had her parents and a good job. My problems were just something she couldn't relate to. Liz had tapered off on contact after I resigned my position, so I didn't have her warm advice or comforting presence anymore. Even when I reached out and texted, she would give me short answers. I had to wonder if she bought into the rumor mill about me, as bizarre as that seemed.

Moreover, Mom was gone, and Tony was too close to my situation to be impartial. That left a handful of girlfriends that I see one in a while, but none that I was tight enough with to reveal the kind of crazy that my life has become. I contacted one when I thought Tony had cancer and was really feeling alone. She was thoughtful and supportive, but she was also in a different phase of her life than I am. I instinctively knew she just wouldn't get it; she would not understand where I was coming from.

Not to mention, I didn't want to burden anyone. The isolation I had sought during my dark years had taken its toll. I fell away from people, and they from me. I was unable to close that gap now. I didn't have a mom or sisters. No best friend or go-to buddy. No work friends to vent with. I was completely alone. Yes, I had Tony and the kids, but a woman needs a kindred woman to talk with. To commiserate with, or bounce ideas off of. Someone whose advice I could soak in. Truthfully, I desperately needed a visit with my therapist, but I couldn't afford it.

When my contract as a Long-Term Sub ended, so did my insurance. I shopped the Marketplace, and the options were dismal. Obamacare is not the savior it was predicted to be. Since I was making less, I had to stick to around a $300 payment per month. I talked to lots of companies, and settled on one that assured me it met my needs. Mind you, I had gone over my med list and doctors with the representative. However, when I went to fill my inhaler, the cost was $600, and my psych meds were $80. How in the hell was I expected to come up with that? There was no money tree in my yard, and no extra in the bank. Lord knows what a therapy appointment would cost, so I didn't bother to schedule one.

Instead, I languished. One morning, I went outside to watch the sunrise. As I did, tears streamed down my face. Why was life so awful anymore? How can I get out of this funk? The world was silent. Even the birds deserted me. There were no answers once again. My mind traveled to the past. I thought about the house I grew up in and how I had always felt safe there, even with a drunk dad. He was just a lovable drunk and helpless to change himself. God knows my mother had given him umpteen chances to. So had his job. In fact, the government paid to send him to rehab multiple times. I can remember talking to him during these stints on the big avocado-green landline. For some reason, it sat on the steps leading upstairs. I would stand and chat with him while I twirled the phone cord. Our conversations always ended with me asking when he would come home, and him answering "soon." What I really should have asked him was when he was going to quit drinking. Yet, I was only a kid and had no idea what was really going on.

By the time I did, he was too far gone. I remembered back to him teaching me to play ball and ride a bike. I also remembered him passed out on the couch, literally "piss drunk." The shame I had felt in that …. I cried harder. I cried for the lost little girl whose father loved alcohol more than he loved her. I cried for the lonely teen whose mother chose a predator for her next husband. I especially bawled for that same teen whose mother turned a blind eye to it all.

When I was done, I felt a great weight lift. Why had I never let all that go? Why hadn't I thought about the broken girl from the broken home? That was where this all started. This was where it had to end.

Chapter 28

While there is great honor and much pride in being a person who can just fight through, I was no longer one of them. I did my best to handle what I could while still practicing self-care, although I loathed being on my own list of things to do. To preserve my sanity, I stepped back from my adult children and let them figure it out. Certainly, I helped when asked, but I left the rest to them. Moreover, Tony and I had used our vacation to reconnect with each other, and our relationship, while strained by finances and such, is in a much better place.

My job search ended when I received an invitation to interview for a school district in a neighboring county. The interview went well, as did the follow-up. I was officially offered the position less than a week before school started. It took almost a week for all of my clearances and references to come back clean. By the time I started, school had already begun. This position was for a gifted teacher of seventh- and eighth-grade students. I had filled a gifted vacancy for the last school district before I became a building sub at their elementary school. That gave me an iota of confidence moving forward.

That was short-lived. This role was a million times more demanding than the past gifted opening I had filled. These kids were next level. This was gifted on steroids! Many were seeking enrichment in Mathematics courses that I had needed a tutor to pass in college. Those with ELA goals were right up my alley, but the Math and Science were going to be a challenge. Luckily, this district was well led, and there were supports put in place for me. Even with those, I was struggling to keep up. This district was super tech-heavy - everything was electronic. Having spent the majority of my career employed by a low-income school district, tech was not my sweet spot.

In fact, I had limited proficiency in many of the apps they were using. Speaking of apps, this district had way more than I had ever worked with or had ever had access to. I didn't know where to start.

Additionally, in-state students who moved into our district with a GIEP, IEP or 504 had to have an initial meeting within the first thirty days of school. There was an influx of them. This meant testing, gathering data, and collecting parent, student, and teacher input, along with a mountain of paperwork for each student. The one thing I felt good about was the paperwork, as I had done this before. Yet, the new school put far more information and projections into theirs. It was next to impossible to get into classrooms and support students amid all this. Parents would soon be complaining if that didn't happen. I tried working from home, but the app used to write the legal documents was notorious for losing its connection. So in essence, you think you have completed everything for a student on your caseload, and you're burned because it ends up missing entire pieces.

As the days plodded on, September gave way to October, and the weather began to cool. Autumn in Pennsylvania is a beautiful sight to behold. The leaves were a riot of colors: gold, amber, pink, scarlet, bright yellow, rust and various tones of orange. I enjoyed the drive from work in the rural county even more now. Some days, I would ride along without music and just soak in the richness of the colors as the sunlight filtered through. At dusk, occasionally, I would lie in bed and watch the cooling fall breeze rustle the branches while a dazzling display of color waved in the wind. I would miss this house when we finally left it, that was for sure. We had so many memories rooted here. After 20 years, they ran almost as deep as the roots of the old oaks outside. I wondered, and not for the first time, what wisdom would trees give if they could speak. Or homes, for that matter. What secrets did the stone, brick and mortar hold? Or harbor? I had spent the darkest days of my life here, and I was eager for a fresh start. Yet, my mom had spent so much time here with us over the years that I knew it was sort of another piece of her I was losing - another tie to my happier past that would be cut.

In October, we applied for a home equity loan to make the necessary repairs and updates to the old girl. That was what I had taken to calling our house. Over the years, I had put a lot of love, sweat, and tears into her, and it felt like saying good-bye to an old friend. One who had watched my kids grow up, and my family grow and dwindle at the same time. *The Circle of Life* from The Lion King has played in my head more than once over the past few weeks. I knew it was time to let it all go and let God guide me to where I was meant to be next. Maybe it was this school, and maybe not. Perhaps that is a stepping stone to something else. It wasn't lost on me that once upon a time, in the not - too-distant past, these thoughts would have had me jumping out of my own skin. I had always been a creature of habit, choosing to lay down roots, traditions and solid ties. I had always wanted a job where I could make a significant difference in improving the world and stay there until retirement. You know Kindreds, the teacher who taught multiple generations of the same family. Someone who was tied to the community she served. That is why what had transpired at my old job was so devastating to me.

Yet, it has taught me valuable lessons. The kind only severe heartbreak and trauma can. Bundle that in with all I learned from losing ma, and I was a completely different person. This monumental change in me had changed my relationships, too. In instances such as Angelica and Aaron, this was a positive change; however, in other relationships, such as my friendships, not so much. The common denominator was pretty obvious. It was me, not them. I had changed so vastly and painfully, I didn't have the interests that I once had. I didn't hold the same things valuable as others did anymore. My frequency has evolved, Kindreds, as vague and odd as it sounds. All of my research and reading has pointed me that way. Meditation has helped, too. My body felt stronger, my mind sounder. This new "enlightenment" cost me much. I wondered if it was a "gift" or just another survival tactic.

Whatever it was, I accepted it, albeit reluctantly. I had never felt this alone in my entire life. I cried about it a lot. Always on the way home from work, though, so I didn't upset anyone else. At

Thanksgiving, life gave me one more major reason to be sorrowful: Tony's mom, Gigi, fell and broke her hip. We had buried Tony's Pop eight months ago. Pop was 97 years old when he died. He had lived a long, fulfilled life. Gigi was mourning him deeply, and this fall didn't help. She spent the holiday in the hospital, but was reportedly in good spirits. That all changed on Black Friday. Gigi had a stroke and was in bad shape. She couldn't really talk or move much. We went and spent Saturday with her at the hospital. She knew we were there and held our hands. I stood next to her, stroking her beautiful, silken silver hair before we left.

"I will see you soon, girlfriend," I said to her, kissing her on the head.

There was a DNR order that Gigi had put in place, and so she went home with hospice. Luckily, her daughter and daughter -in-law were both nurses. This was the DIL who had lost her husband the year that we lost my mom. They gave Gigi a warm bath and a massage, then transferred her to her waiting bed with fresh sheets. I can only imagine how relaxing that was for Gigi and how good she must have felt being clean in her own bed after the prolonged hospital stay. I also imagine it was healing for my sister-in-law to care for her late husband's mother in her final days.

On Monday, Gigi's remaining sorority sisters came to say goodbye. These women had been friends for over 80 years. I am in awe of that - what a bond! I only wish for friends like that, but everyone probably does. These women lived it. There is a picture of all seven of them at the beach, the summer they graduated high school - 1949, I believe. That black-and-white photo was chosen for the remembrance cards and for her obituary as well. Gigi passed late that night, in her own home, after leading a life of service and love to her family. She was an amazing woman, always positive and happy. I would miss her terribly. She was like my second mom.

Understandably, Tony took her death hard. He had just lost Pop eight months ago, now Gigi. Plus, she had seemed more like her old self at our last visit, which was the week before she fell. Tony, Kaleb and I went to see her and Pop every month for years. Then it was only Gigi we were visiting. As I said, she had grieved hard. Who could blame her? They were married for over 70 years. Yet, that was the cruelest part-she seemed better at our last visit, and it gave us hope that she was coming around.

Now the last is gone. The last of our "great generation." I knew the intense pain Tony was feeling, but I couldn't lessen it. All I could do was be there for him. He stayed out of work and just languished as I did. I let him; I knew he needed the time to process, grieve and heal. The funeral was beautiful, and a large congregation gathered to say goodbye. At the luncheon after, all the dishes served had Gigi- or Mom-themed names. It was a lovely tribute to a woman full of grace and class. She and Pop had raised eight kids and had thirteen grandchildren, three great-grandchildren, and even a great-great-grandson. They had buried four of their own children and still carried on with dignity and love. The mark of a truly well-lived life. Plus, they had many waiting for them on the other side.

Still, it was little comfort to Tony, who had Christmas to contend with a few weeks later. He still hadn't returned to work, but had gone to the family doctor. He was just waiting to feel better, to come out from under the veil of heavy grieving. It was much like depression, wherein your body hurts, you are dizzy and groggy. Your head feels full of something, but it sure ain't brains because you can't function proper or make decisions. It is sort of like sleepwalking through pain. The doctor thought similarly, so Tony muddled on, crying, cleaning and turning inwards. I guess it helped to have a spouse who had experienced this before, but I wish there was more I could have done for him.

When Christmas came, he didn't want to open gifts or get out of bed. I let him sleep in and set about making a scaled-back Christmas brunch. Once upon a time, we would have been entertaining my mom and step dad, Gigi, Pop, my brothers and even my Nan back in the day.

We loved Christmas, but it just didn't hold the same joy for us anymore. Tony got that now. He had said to me the week before, "Now I get why you didn't want to celebrate Christmas that first year after your mom died."

Still, you carry on, because honestly, what choice do we have? I made some breakfast casseroles, and my brother and his wife brought bagels. We were sitting at the dining room table, talking about how much we missed Mom when Jocely popped in with a tray of Christmas goodies. I was so thankful, and it felt good to know we weren't forgotten. Tony stayed in bed all day. There was never a Christmas that felt less Christmasy to me.

During brunch, Angelica called, screaming and crying. She and baby daddy had decided to call it quits and were trying to live out the lease before they went their separate ways. Well, it wasn't working because the week before, he had broken her wrist. She was now serving tables with a soft cast and trying to care for a toddler. Tony wanted to take all of his anger about losing his mom out on Kaleb's dad, but he didn't. He knew that was a slippery slope that would lead to him being in jail. Ang ended up coming here until she could get him out. It took a PFA, but he finally left. She and Kaleb went back after she had the locks changed. That didn't stop him, though. There were threats and harassment back and forth on both sides. The hatred and rage turning into abuse went both ways, but I just wanted to stay out of it and take care of Kaleb, but I kept getting sucked in. Finally, a judge upheld the PFA and told them to work out custodial visits or go to custody court. It seemed as if it would work at first, but in the end their vitriol for each other won out. And Kaleb lost.

Chapter 29

After a month, Tony returns to work, but his heart just isn't in it anymore. His work had not sent a card, flowers, or anything. No acknowledgement of losing your mother, but when are you coming back to work? In fact, not many bereavement messages came at all. We just don't have the tribe we used to. It hurts, but it is real. Tony floundered through the stages of grieving. It is an awkward, painful process made worse by the fact that you never knew how you would feel or react to people or events.

One morning, we were at the cabin and decided to venture out for breakfast. It was crowded, so we sat at the counter. Tony seemed really fidgety and uncomfortable. At one point, he leaned over and said to me, "Why does everyone keep looking at me?"

"They know you are changing," I replied. "They can sense something about you: tragedy, sorrow, something," I added, remembering back to when it was me at stores, and people were looking at me all the time like I knew some big secret. He didn't take the attention well, and we headed back home.

Meanwhile, Baby Daddy was at the apartment he wasn't supposed to be at, and he ended up getting arrested after threatening Angelica. Since he wasn't stable enough to have Kaleb, Tony, Ella, and me became the primary caregivers when Ang couldn't. It is a lot. My almost -55-year-old body has trouble keeping up. Add in that the knees are starting up again, and I am back to being exhausted and in pain. The knee shots aren't doing the trick for me anymore. My knees are just too far gone.

In January, Trump was elected President. He starts off with sweeping legislation that rolls the clock back a bit. Plus, he begins investigating government waste and fraud. It is not America's finest hour. The amount of money being sent abroad to pay for ridiculous things is mind-boggling. Meanwhile, at home, our own citizens suffer. I tend to agree with Kurt Vonnegut, who said, "We'll go down as the first society that wouldn't save itself because it wasn't cost-effective."

It felt as if we were all living in a bad reality TV show, universally. Iran had been bombing Israel, too. Russia was still attempting to annex Ukraine, and one had to wonder how the rest of the world was coming to terms with him being back in office. Trump was feared, so things in the Middle East started to settle down a tiny bit. One thing was for certain: the foreign aid would stop. I had mixed feelings on this because Southerners are still suffering immensely here at home. I have seen the devastation and families living in tents. I am not saying other countries don't need help; I am saying we should be helping our own people first. Then the others. The nuns always told us, "Charity begins at home."

Speaking of which, doesn't it make you wonder if this is the beginning of the end times, Kindreds? The world is in an absolute state of disorder. Not to mention what we have done to nature and our environment. Who would have ever thought micro plastics would embed themselves in our systems? There is a huge imbalance currently, and it touches far more than just politics and economics. The energy is all off.

Since I am ending on a rant, I will give you one more morsel of food for thought: how about the other members of NATO stand up and take some responsibility instead of just expecting the US to bail everyone out? We can't be the saviors of the world if we don't save ourselves. Trump is leaving NATO, apparently. Will he turn the US into an isolationist nation? I don't know, but isolation didn't do me any favors, and I sincerely doubt it will help us globally in the long run.

Ordinarily, this would have kept me up at night, but not with this job and watching Kaleb. I was plum tuckered out by bedtime. These little blessings do not go unacknowledged. Sometimes that is what carries us through a rough day - simply being still and in the moment, feeling gratitude. I term it the "Flip of the Script."

Perhaps it is walking briskly to the local coffee shop during lunch break, or practicing breathing in your car before going to work. A long shower, naps, podcasts, meditation, gardening, baking, reading or writing for pleasure, even recalling a happy memory - whatever it takes to keep you here. Our response is the only thing we can control in this out -of-control, over -the-top world. It sucks, and I hate it, but there it is.

Some days, I still cry on the way home from work. I feel so lonely, even when surrounded by people. I miss my mom unendingly, and I want my old life back. Alas, not possible, and I realize it. I loathe it, but accept it very begrudgingly. Then I acknowledge how I feel, why I feel that way, and what I can do about it. If the answer is nothing, I pray on it. I may make a prosperity simmer pot, meditate, do some cleaning, or sage. Anything to make me feel like I am taking control of my own life again. Even if that equates to a nap, I listen to my body and only take on what I can reasonably handle. I have learned to ignore the dust and the dirt, something old Jen would have been aghast at. I won't go so far as to say I embrace it, but I accept that with dogs and a grandchild, the house will never stay clean. And that's okay. I am managing life's curve balls by minimizing damage where and when I can. The rest, well, let's just say I give it to God. I let myself be guided by my gifts, my heart, and my mind, coupled with extensive research and prayer. I still believe my ancestors are protecting me, and I hope my ways honor them. I now feel ready to handle life in a way that allows for joy, not just sorrow.

Currently, we are packing and purging. The purge is also self-care. It is very empowering to break free from the boxes and other items that hold us down. It is creating open spaces in our home that make me feel less heavy. The construction on our house begins in two weeks. I am scouring the internet for a one-floor home closer to my work for us to purchase. It is not an easy task. Prices are still insane.

While the world continues to burn, I plug along. At a much slower rate than ever before, but progress is still progress, even when done in baby steps. I still stay away from network news, and it is finally being revealed that they take kickbacks and all other sorts of violations that should never be. The major news outlets are being unmasked, and it is being proven that they had an agenda all along. Only the Sheeple should be shocked by this.

Although I may not be a direct supporter of Trump, it wasn't lost on me how much he was shaking up the old-world order. I should have been mind blown by what he was uncovering, but my jaded self couldn't muster even that. None is to be trusted, and I have said it before. Still, it was fun to watch and read about the career-long politicians who were shaking in their Gucci loafers. Everything was going to come out now: how corrupt our government is, how they divert funds to pet projects and fail the average citizen repeatedly. Perhaps we will find out who is a pedophile, who is backing foreign wars and how our government ended up being an archaic system that requires an overhaul. If Trump is good at anything, it's following the money trail. It will all come out. The illusion is crumbling, and the facade of the old power systems is cracking under pressure. Will these events create a better America? Will it restore us to our former glory? I don't have those answers, but one thing is certain - This will forever change who we are as a society. It is up to us, the citizens, to make ourselves better. To do better, to be better. Whatever it takes, because in the end, that is what this wild, wacky world is about: evolving into the best form you can, using all the tools you can find.

Peace out.
February 17, 2025
Media, Pa.

Appendix

*Kindreds, this is by no means meant to be an exhaustive list of mental health resources. If you or someone you know needs help, this is at least a place to start. **You matter**, and the world needs us, so if you are struggling right now, please reach out.*

National Institute on Mental Health. www.nimh.nih.org

The CDC has solid resources for many different demographics: www.cdc.gov

National Alliance on Mental Illness: https://www.nami.org

International Society for Suicide Prevention: call or text 988. There is also a chat feature available.

Veterans Crisis Line: dial 988 and press 1, text 838255 or go to: https://mentalhealth.va.gov

National Action Alliance for Suicide Prevention: https://theactionalliance.org

Mayo Clinic www.mayoclininc.org

American Psychological Association: https://www.apa.org

American Psychiatric Association: https://www.psychiatry.org

Find resources, doctors and practitioners of mental health by visiting Psychology Today:

https://www.psychologytoday.com